Business School

Book 2
Managing retail stores

Prepared by Fiona Ellis-Chadwick, Caroline Emberson and Diane Preston

This publication forms part of the Open University module B122 An Introduction to Retail Management and Marketing. Details of this and other Open University modules can be obtained from the Student Registration and Enquiry Service, The Open University, PO Box 197, Milton Keynes MK7 6BJ, United Kingdom (tel. +44 (0)845 300 60 90; email general-enquiries@open.ac.uk).

Alternatively, you may visit the Open University website at www.open.ac.uk where you can learn more about the wide range of modules and packs offered at all levels by The Open University.

To purchase a selection of Open University module materials visit www.ouw.co.uk, or contact Open University Worldwide, Walton Hall, Milton Keynes MK7 6AA, United Kingdom for a brochure (tel. +44 (0)1908 858793; fax +44 (0)1908 858787; email ouw-customer-services@open.ac.uk).

The Open University Walton Hall, Milton Keynes MK7 6AA

First published 2011

Edited and designed by The Open University.

Typeset in India by OKS Prepress Services, Chennai.

Printed in the United Kingdom by Cambrian Printers, Aberystwyth.

FSC

Mixed Sources

Product group from well-managed forests and other controlled sources

Cert no. TT-COC-2200
www.fsc.org
© 1996 Forest Stewardship Council

ISBN 978 1 7800 7311 8

2.1

Contents

Introduction to Book 2

Welcome to Book 2, which explores different elements of managing a retail store. In this book we look at some of the key skills needed by store managers. These include managing the overall customer experience, dealing with the administrative and communications side of the operation and taking responsibility for the motivation and performance of staff. By exploring some aspects of the human resource management (HRM) function, we see that a key part of a store manager's role is to ensure that the store has the right staff with the right skills to make it run successfully. We also look at other important aspects of managing retail stores such as merchandising, stock management and managing shoppers and customer service. Introducing you to these ideas is intended to enhance your understanding of retail management at an operational level.

You need to allow about ten hours' reading and activity time for each of the four study sessions covered in this book. This includes taking part in your tutor group forum (TGF).

As with Block 1 there are three study elements for you to work on:

- Multimedia activities 2 focus on practical issues that affect the management of retail store operations. Please note, you should study this part of the block before completing the study materials in this book. If you have not done so already, visit the B122 website and complete Multimedia activities 2.

- Book 2 focuses on ideas and theories that should help you to understand more about the behaviour of retail managers, employees and customers and is an important part of becoming an effective retail operations manager.

- The tutor group forum (TGF) gives you an opportunity to share your viewpoints. Please note that in Blocks 2–4 your contribution to the TGF forms part of the assessment for each of these blocks, so it is important to take part in forum discussions. We also hope that you find that you enjoy and learn from the views and experiences of other students.

It is important to complete each element of Block 2 before moving on to Block 3. Each part of the block should make a unique contribution to your understanding of store operations management.

Book 2 consists of four study sessions:

Session 2: Aspects of a retail manager's role

Session 3: Managing the workforce

Session 4: Managing customers

Session 5: Managing a retail store

In Block 1 we began by thinking about the meaning of retailing and why we buy certain products. As an introduction to this book, let's focus on why we might choose to visit particular stores and the experiences we have when we are in the store. An overall, positive experience for the customer is clearly a key objective of managing a retail store. So, to start, try to picture a shop that you like to visit, then consider why you go there, and what it is that attracts you to go to that particular shop rather than any other.

On a recent, trip to Istanbul, I visited the spice market and found the shops and stalls fascinating. What amazed me the most, from a store operations viewpoint, was not only the amount of merchandise on sale, but also the neatness of all of the stores. The image above is a picture of a store in the spice market selling carpets, kilims (tapestry woven rugs), silks, cashmere, jewellery, and oils. I observed the two men working in the shop (in the picture) for a while before entering. They were constantly tidying, organising and replacing the merchandise for sale as well as attending to every customer's needs, by presenting and offering products for customers to examine.

This was a very exotic location but the helpfulness of the people in-store, their level of knowledge of the products and the way in which their shops are managed are all very important criteria that I and millions of shoppers use to inform our choice of shopping destination. I hope this example helps you to get a feel for the kind of issues regarding managing a retail store that we are going to be exploring in the rest of this book.

Learning outcomes

The main aims of Block 2 are to introduce some key aspects of managing day-to-day retail store operations. The focus is on the management of the workforce, customers, stores and stock. The key objectives of Book 2 are to:

- develop your understanding of the roles and responsibilities of different types of retail managers
- explore different ways of organising and managing a retail store
- identify the key issues that affect human resource management in retailing
- consider how important it is for retail managers to understand shopper behaviour and levels of customer service
- identify and consider the activities that are involved in managing a store.

Session 2 Aspects of a retail manager's role

This session explores what it takes to manage a retail store. From the very smallest business operated by a sole trader to the largest retail corporation, there are some core principles of general retail management which, if applied correctly, can improve the effectiveness of the retail operation. We are going to examine some key issues and ideas and begin by looking at the general nature of management in retailing, the role of the store manager and the skills and additional management techniques, which help managers operate stores successfully.

2.1 What are we managing?

It should be noted that some retailers appear to focus more on the products than the people involved in the retailer operation, and the levels of service can seem very limited, for most of these retailers this is a strategic move.

What is involved in retail management? Before we can fully answer this question, we need to think about what is being managed. For many decades, retailers have focused most of their attention on managing products (merchandise). Simplistically, this approach led to the growth in importance of the functions of buying, logistics (e.g., getting the goods to the store) and merchandising (e.g., store layout, fittings and product displays). However, since the mid-1950s, as retail industries in developed nations began to rapidly expand, competition has intensified. The result is that retailers have tended to become strategic in the ways they manage their operations. In practical terms, this means working out ways to differentiate the retail offering from that of competitors by improving a customer's experience in the store. This shift in focus from products to customers dictates a key part of managing modern retail stores, namely: the customer experience and the staff who are involved in delivering the customer service.

Aldi, Lidl and many other discount supermarkets offer limited customer service and limited ranges of products at very low prices. This is a strategic choice to meet the needs of certain sectors of the grocery market.

In Block 1 we learnt about the concept of customer value and the importance of understanding and satisfying customer needs. Do you remember how customer value meant different things to different people and that retailers create value by devising a particular customer experience through the products they sell and the services they offer? Now we can begin to think about the actual management implications and how retailers not only manage the products they sell but also manage the workforce that provides the additional services associated with product sales and creates unique customer experiences. For example, the management team at Sainsbury's store in Hazel Grove, Stockport employed a team of customer ambassadors who patrol the aisles looking for ways to help shoppers, by guiding them to the products they are looking for and providing additional help and advice in order to enhance the customer experience.

Activity 2.1 Managing the customer experience

Spend about 30 minutes on this activity.

Purpose: to think about the differences in the customer experience at an individual family-owned store and a store owned by a large corporation.

Task:

(a) Imagine you are the store manager of an independent retail store like the one shown in the image above, you have three staff and sell speciality products (in this case, handmade chocolates).

Suggest three aspects of the customers' experience you would expect your staff to provide.

1

2

3

Drugstore is a term that is widely used in North America to denote a retail store which mainly sells pharmacy products and medicines.

(b) Now imagine you are a store manager of a branch of Walgreens Drugstores. Walgreens is the largest drugstore chain in the USA, with over 6,300 stores, selling cosmetics, pharmacy products and a wide range of other consumer goods associated with health and well being. How do you think the customer experience varies between the Chocolat shop and a Walgreens store?

(c) What do you think are the most important skills you would need to be able to manage either of these stores?

Feedback

(a) I would want the staff to:

1   offer a very personal and friendly customer service

2   be very knowledgeable about the quality and the ingredients of the products

3   be committed to the company because they enjoy their work.

You may have suggested many other valid aspects. The important point to reflect on is the extent to which you feel that your management strategy for the staff might ensure a good customer experience, which would encourage customers to return to the store.

(b) The experience in the Chocolat shop is likely to involve a more personal interaction but we can only surmise whether it will be a good or bad experience. It is easy to imagine that visiting a large Walgreens store would be an impersonal experience, however, you might be interested to note that even though Walgreens is a very large retail corporation, customer service is central to the company's strategy. Indeed, when Charles R Walgreen opened his first drugstore in Chicago in 1901, his aims were to provide superb customer service and a selection of products that customers really wanted and, perhaps most importantly, knowledgeable staff who were totally committed to providing genuine value to the customer. Perhaps the biggest challenge was how to retain these management principles as the business grew from a single store just like the Chocolat shop to a multinational chain of retail drugstores. Walgreen is said to have succeeded in addressing this challenge by sticking to and practicing what he preached and focusing on the customer experience.

Walgreen was a retail pioneer; he instituted a change in levels of service and personal attention that was unequalled by virtually any other pharmacy in Chicago. These founding principles went on to drive the growth of the company and continue to be central to the business strategy today.

(c) The types of skills you might have in your list are the ability to:

- **organise the staff, the stock and the store** – this is a difficult balance and would clearly depend on the size, context and type of retail organisation
- **make decisions** – about all sorts of things, like which staff to employ and the other aspects of managing a retail store that we will be covering in this block

- **communicate with staff** – not least, making sure that they know what is expected of them – a key skill in any type of manager's job
- **motivate staff** – help them see that what they do contributes to the success of the store
- **be self-motivated** – which probably means having clear objectives for yourself and having the opportunity to develop the skills and knowledge needed to achieve them
- **be a good leader** – definitions of a leader or a 'good' leader vary in academic literature but we would probably all agree that there are key characteristics. Perhaps you can think about the sort of things you would define as good leadership based on your own life and work experiences, both in a retail context and elsewhere.

Perhaps the most important point to note here is that, whatever the size of the retail operation, managing the store, the products and the workforce in order to deliver the right customer experience is central to becoming successful in retail operations management. Next let's look in more detail at some key skills that might be needed by the manager of a retail store.

2.2 Some skills of the store manager

The store manager's role involves organising human resources (staff) and the physical aspects of the store (such as stock) in effective ways to meet strategic and tactical objectives. For example, a grocery retailer's marketing strategy may have set out a longer-term strategic objective to introduce new organic products throughout its stores in order to attract new customers. The store manager is likely to be responsible for implementing changes at the store level that will contribute to the achievement of the strategic objective. To be able to do this effectively the manager will need skills such as being able to make decisions, build teams, communicate and take an overview of the wider impact of the changes on the store. They will also need to consider the impact of changes at the local level and respond to any reactions to the changes.

Cox and Brittain (2003, pp. 208–9) suggest the types of skills that (retail) managers need will include:

- administrative
- decisional (problem-solving)
- communication
- motivation

In the following sections we will look at each one of these in turn.

Administrative skills

One of the most important administrative abilities in managing the operational aspects of a store is planning and organising events in advance. Having sufficient and appropriate merchandise to meet customer demand is critical to the success of the operation. So a manager will be required to plan stock requirements and the frequency at which stock is replenished. Additionally, a manager will need to manage the workforce and be able to delegate specific tasks to individuals, for example; replenishing stock, updating point-of-sale materials and dealing with customer complaints. Another important skill is monitoring compliance, in other words checking to make sure that instructions have been understood and implemented correctly. There are administrative elements to most parts of a retail manager's role.

Decisional (problem-solving) skills

According to Cox and Brittain, (2003, 208–9), there are five key problem-solving skills in retail management:

1 **judgement** – being able to arrive at appropriate decisions and conclusions (which are in line with company policy and strategic aims) using available information resources.

2 **problem analysis** – being able to identify the source of problems or issues and assess their nature and scope.

3 **decision making** – being able to select the most appropriate option from a range of choices.

4 **innovation** – being able to think outside the box and identify new ways to solve old problems.

5 **creativity** – being aware of what is happening in the store and in the sector, watching for any changes taking place and having the ability to respond and formulate general management principles.

Communication skills

Communication skills are important in all occupations, and no less so in a retail management context. Basically, communication is about sending and receiving messages, but, for this to be effective, understanding has to occur between the sender and receiver of the message. In retailing, internal communications can take place on different levels. For example; the senior management team makes strategic decisions, which are then communicated down through the organisation; when a customer makes a complaint, the message is likely to be passed up through the organisation; at a regional management meeting ideas may be communicated laterally between regional managers. You will learn more about how theoretical models of communication inform the development of external marketing communications in Block 3.

According to Cox and Brittain (2003), there are four key skills a manager needs to communicate effectively:

1 Actively listening and interpreting messages. This is probably the most important communication skill.

2 Ability to participate in a dialogue when communicating with small groups of staff and customers. This skill is important as it creates an opportunity to gauge reactions and respond appropriately. There can be a tendency, particularly if the message is complex or has negative connotations, to allow communication to be a monologue (one-sided) rather than a dialogue.

3 Ability to present ideas in a clear and appropriate manner. A retail manager will need to be able to present ideas to the workforce in the store as well as to the regional and senior management teams.

4 Effective writing skills. At various times the manager will need to write a range of written communication forms such as reports and internal memos.

In addition to these skills, a manager should also be aware of the different channels of communication by which to send and receive information. We can use the next activity to help us think about this.

Activity 2.2 Channels of communication

Spend about 10 minutes on this activity.

Purpose: to identify the types of communication you might encounter as a retail manager.

Task: Think about attending an Open University tutorial, then make a list of the different types of communication you might encounter.

Feedback

There are four main types of communication you might encounter in this context:

1 **verbal and oral** – face-to-face communications, tutor group discussions, live online discussions

2 **written** – handouts, lecture notes, books

3 **visual** – videos, posters, PowerPoint presentations, online films

4 **non-verbal** – body language, the face and body movements of tutors and students.

Retail managers should be aware of, and able to interpret, different forms of personal communication if they are to make informed decisions about how to respond to them. Good communication skills are important for retail managers as they need to, for example, motivate staff and bring about change and improvement.

Various barriers to communication are likely to stop a message being fully understood:

1 **Poor communication** – messages should be clear, understandable, accurate, and to the point. Vague and rambling messages can lead to confusion, misunderstanding, tension and conflict.

2 **Information processing** – as individuals we process and interpret messages and then store them in memory for later use. According to Jobber (2010, p. 123), 'Two key aspects of information processing are perception and learning. Perception is the complex process by which people select, organise, and interpret sensory stimulation into a meaningful picture of the world'. However, from a communication perspective we need to be aware that there are three underlying processes that can act as barriers to communication:

(i) Selective attention – the process by which we filter and block things that are not meaningful to us and or are not consistent with our current experiences and beliefs

(ii) Selective distortion – this happens when we shape and mould information to fit our existing experiences and beliefs

(iii) Selective retention – we have a habit of only remembering messages that fit our existing experiences and beliefs, which can seriously affect the communication process.

The retail manager has to understand how individuals process information and may suggest training and workshops to help with information processing in order to improve communication within the workforce.

3 **Communication structures** – as organisations grow, gaps can occur in lines of communication. Additionally, store managers can become very busy, particularly at certain times of the retail trading year, which can mean communications get less effective. A good manager needs to be aware of how messages move through the organisation and find ways to repair breaks in the system.

Motivational skills

Motivational skills are very important when managing a retail operation as it is crucial to have the ability to encourage and guide the workforce towards the achievement of common goals, such as achieving the weekly sales target. Store managers are leaders of the workforce in their stores and are likely to use a range of motivational techniques to increase performance and help employees achieve personal goals and targets. This includes matching the right person to the right job and making that job as interesting as possible. We will look at this idea (socio-technical design) a little later on.

Research has suggested that there is a clear link between effective management of staff, high levels of job satisfaction and loyalty to an organisation. Therefore, it is important for managers to understand the ideas that underpin motivation if they are to motivate their workforce successfully. Let's take a brief look at some of the key theories that have influenced ideas about motivation.

Maslow, (1943) linked the needs of humans to the way individuals behave. He developed his theories into five categories of needs, which potentially motivate individual behaviour:

1 **Physiological needs** – if we are hungry or thirsty we will actively seek food and drink in order to satisfy ourselves and if we are cold, we seek a source of warmth.

2 **Security needs** – we like to feel safe, to have job security and financial stability.

3 **Social needs** – we want friendship and companionship with others and to feel we belong.

4 **Esteem or Status needs** – we like to be able to make a valuable contribution to a group and being recognised as having done so.

5 **Self-fulfilment needs** – we want to develop as an individual to our fullest potential. This is quite a difficult concept but it basically means: having had all our physical and social needs met, we are then motivated by 'higher level' factors such as the chance to be creative or to have autonomy in our job.

Maslow presented his ideas about motivation as a pyramid or hierarchy as shown in figure 2.1. The main inference is that low-level needs have to be satisfied before an individual will be motivated to pursue the next level need.

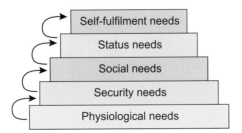

Figure 2.1 Maslow's hierarchy of needs shows a progression of motivating factors

Maslow's hierarchy of needs theory provided a springboard for Frederick Herzberg et al (1959) to investigate motivation in the workplace further. He termed the elements of work connected to the job environment 'hygiene factors'. These factors included pay and working conditions, company policies, and the physical environment where the individuals were working. He found that if the hygiene factors are poor, the workers tended to be dissatisfied with their jobs and were generally suffering from demotivation. He proposed that improving the hygiene factors (for instance, increasing levels of pay) might reduce *demotivation* but would not succeed in *motivating* the workforce as might be expected. The things that were motivators, Herzberg suggested, were aspects of the job itself such as increased responsibility, interesting and challenging work.

Figure 2.2 links together Maslow's needs theory and Herzberg's motivational theory. It is important to note that hygiene factors are most likely to act as dissatisfiers. In other words, if, for example, pay and working conditions are not to a level that an employee expects, the outcome will be dissatisfaction.

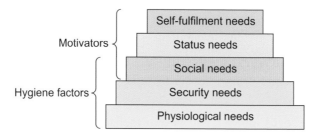

Figure 2.2 Needs, motivations and hygiene factors

Following these theories, managers wishing to motivate the workforce should focus their attention on how to align motivators with higher-level needs. For example, setting objectives that are appropriate to the skill level of the individual should allow achievement of goals. Increased responsibility could enable individuals to feel they are making a valuable contribution. Creating interesting and challenging work should give an opportunity for individuals to take ownership of tasks and at the same time feel a sense of belonging.

Box 2.1 Theories X and Y

Douglas McGregor's work in the 1960s and beyond put forward two theories:

Theory X suggests that individuals actually avoid work and without active intervention by management, the workforce would be passive and even resistant to what their employer is asking them to do. Working on this premise, staff must be persuaded, rewarded, even punished if managers are to modify their work behaviour. The resulting X Theory management style is authoritarian.

Theory Y is based on a different set of assumptions about human nature and motivation. Individuals are not seen as passive or resistant but as having the potential for development and a capacity for assuming responsibility. This theory suggests that it is the responsibility of management to make it possible for people to recognise and develop these human characteristics for themselves. Moreover, managers should seek to arrange organisational conditions and methods of operation so that people can best achieve their own goals by directing their efforts towards organisational objectives.

(Source: McGregor, 1989, p. 321)

The important point to take from these motivational theories is that different ideas and assumptions about individuals and their needs and capabilities will affect how a manager works with his/her staff. All of the skills considered so far (administrative, decisional, communication and motivation skills) underpin the activities of a retail manager.

You might want to give some more thought to how the types of theories and issues we have discussed here work within a retail context – what issues will be more prevalent and how, for example, would you motivate staff within different types of retail environment?

2.3 Job design

The next section looks at how retail managers might improve performance and motivate staff by thinking about the job itself. This is the socio-technical approach to job design that assumes that equal attention is paid to the design of the tasks people do as to the needs of the people themselves. Roberts explained this as follows:

> … a lot of the problems of motivation fall away when someone is well-matched to the job they are doing. In such circumstances working hard and performing well happens simply because it is rewarding and satisfying.

Roberts, 2007, p. 50

In 1980 Hackman and Oldham developed a job characteristics model and argued that, in order to enhance their feelings of responsibility, an employee's job needs to involve substantial freedom, autonomy and discretion in how it is carried out. According to this model, only when all three of these aspects are present will an employee feel that outcomes are the result of their own efforts and therefore something for which they have personal responsibility.

In the USA, Anderson (1984) tested Hackman and Oldham's model in a study of independent food group retailers in Illinois. She explored how job characteristics of supervisors and clerks were related to their job satisfaction, absenteeism and job performance. She surveyed 171 people working in four departments (meat, produce, grocery and delicatessen) across five different stores. Whilst she found that there was no significant relationship between any of these job characteristics and absenteeism, the responses suggested that there was a relationship between the extent of autonomy and feedback and the employees' overall job satisfaction and job performance.

Her results are interesting because of the links between autonomy, feedback and job performance. These dimensions accounted for 5–6 per cent of the differences in employees' work performance. This finding led Anderson to conclude that:

> … retail food store managers should allow plenty of opportunity for employees to decide when and how to implement certain tasks. The work itself should provide feedback to the employees so that they will know how they are doing on the job – there should be tangible outcomes that can be associated with a particular employee's efforts.

(Anderson 1984, pp. 15–16)

Activity 2.3 Job design and job satisfaction

Spend about 20 minutes on this activity.

Purpose: to consider how intrinsic job satisfaction and job performance might be improved.

Task:

(a) Based on Anderson's (1984) findings in the US retail food industry, how might in-store replenishment operations in a local supermarket be redesigned to improve intrinsic job satisfaction and job performance for the people doing these tasks?

(b) From your own experience or observations, to what extent do you believe changes to the design of this type of work are practical and/or desirable? (Consider your answers to this second question from the perspective of both the store manager and the employee tasked to carry out the job.)

Feedback

(a) In her study, Anderson (1984) found that two main elements seemed to improve employees' intrinsic job satisfaction and job performance. Employees with the autonomy to decide how to carry out their assigned tasks and received feedback on their performance were more satisfied than those who simply received feedback from their manager.

(b) I thought of a number of ways in which in-store replenishment operations might be designed to provide greater intrinsic job satisfaction. Employees could be given responsibility to ensure adequate levels of on-shelf availability for a particular section of the store (e.g., a category such as frozen food). Feedback on this area (and therefore, indirectly, on their performance) could be provided in the form of the sales figures for that category for the employee's shift. The employee could also be given the autonomy to decide the sequence in which products in the relevant aisle should be replenished. In this way, they could see which products were selling fastest and therefore make any necessary adjustments to their replenishment schedules. (You will look in more detail at how merchandising and replenishment tasks of this type are actually carried out in Session 4.)

From an employee's perspective, a task of this nature will place greater demands on their abilities than simply following the sequence and replenishment instructions given by a section manager or determined automatically by an in-store information system. This may lead to increased levels of social interaction between employees, which some people may prefer. As we stated earlier, Hackman and Oldham's model is a socio-technical job characteristics model and these points illustrate the social aspects of their ideas.

From the perspective of a retail store manager, however, this type of work design may raise planning and operational issues. These are the technical aspects of work identified by Hackman and Oldham. The manager may wish to direct employees to work flexibly between sections, for example, to cover for absent colleagues. As you may know, in many large supermarkets these functions are managed centrally. When employees carry out pre-planned replenishment sequences, inadequacies in restocking and shelf planning policies may be revealed.

So we might say that in terms of the retail manager and her/his staff – and between any individual and their employing organisation – there is an agreement or contract. From a formal point of view there is written job contract setting out terms and conditions, but there is also a mutual, implicit, usually unwritten understanding that both parties have of each other; often called a psychological contract.

To provide some examples, a retail manager (representing the organisation), might expect that people come to work on time and are appropriately dressed, that they will try their hardest to contribute to a positive customer experience, that they may well have to stay a little later sometimes and/or help their colleagues to ensure that a good job gets done.

Employees on the other hand would, for instance, expect their working environment to be safe, that there would not be any type of discrimination in terms of recruitment and promotion, that they would not be asked to work unreasonable hours or to perform tasks that they were unable to or that would put them in a uncomfortable situation. Let's explore the psychological contract idea in a bit more depth using the activity below.

Activity 2.4 Employer/employee relationships

Spend about 20 minutes on this activity.

Purpose: to map out what a member of the workforce might expect to give to an employer and what they might expect in return.

Task: Imagine you are working for a large grocery retailer such as Tesco, Sainsbury's, or Morrisons as a store manager. Use your own work experiences, either voluntary or paid, to fill in Table 2.1(a) The psychological contract.

In the column headed 'Inputs' make a list of all of the things you might bring to your working life (inputs to the businesses), hours worked, loyalty to the company, etc. In the column headed 'Rewards', make a list of the rewards you might receive from your employer such as responsibility, personal development, etc.

Table 2.1(a) The psychological contract

Work (inputs)	Rewards

Feedback

Table 2.1(b) gives a list of the kinds of inputs you might have come up with.

Table 2.1(b) The psychological contract

Work (inputs)	Rewards
Time	Job security
Flexibility	Good working conditions
Hours	Training
Effort	Personal development
Ideas and innovation	Promotion
Hard work	Awards and pay increments
Trust	Pension
Loyalty	Retirement planning
Commitment	Challenging and interesting work
Goal achievement	Safe working environment
Acceptance	Travel
Respect	Mutual respect
Change	Acceptable workload
Management skills	Equity
Energy and enthusiasm	Power and influence

If the psychological contract is broken by either party there is likely to be a negative impact on job satisfaction and on the commitment of the employee to the organisation.

2.4 Conclusions

Session 2 started by considering some of the key aspects of a store manager's role and providing more detail on the types of motivational theories that can influence the style of management. Approaches towards the management of the workforce are constantly evolving in response to an ever-changing business environment.

In the retail sector there is often high staff turnover, and it is often difficult to recruit good staff due to low average wages, long working hours and relatively poor working conditions. This is clearly not the case in all retail organisations and some companies like Marks and Spencer and Walmart are famous for their prioritisation of HRM and positive working conditions.

Whichever standpoint an organisation adopts with regard to HRM, every retailer has to make important decisions that come under an HRM umbrella. For example, HRM teams, store and section managers are faced daily with decisions about how many staff are needed to make the organisation function effectively; how to divide the in-store tasks, so that stores provide the experience the customer expects; and the training needs of individual employees which will enable each individual to perform at their best.

In the retail sector there have been several significant changes in recent years which have affected working patterns such as liberalisation of opening hours and Sunday trading. As a result, many individuals are part-time workers or work flexible hours; there is less job security; technology is changing the nature of the work and organisational structures are becoming more fluid. These are all factors that have an impact on everyone in the workforce at whatever level they are employed. In the next session we will explore some more ideas and practices involved in the management of staff within a store.

Learning outcomes

When you have completed all the study elements for this session, you should be able to:

- identify and explain the range of skills a manager might need to manage a retail store operation successfully
- explain some key concepts of motivation and job design that might be used to design jobs and enhance the commitment of retail employees.
- describe the idea of a psychological contract between employer and employee and why this is important
- use your own experiences to learn about retail management.

You should also have developed your learning by completing the activities and reflections in this study session.

Session 3 Managing the workforce

In this study session we look at a key business function, human resource management (HRM) and the types of activities HRM (sometimes called Personnel) is responsible for. The HRM department will be different in different types of retail operation; it may be a large, centralised department function or in some cases just one individual responsible for matters concerning the workforce. Sometimes HRM policies and procedures might be contracted out to a different company. HRM issues may certainly take more or less priority depending on the history and culture of an organisation. However the HRM function is operated within a retail organisation, it is clear that HRM activities and issues and managing the workforce will form an important part of any retail manager's job.

3.1 The complexity of retail roles

Let's look first at an unusual career opportunity in the retailing sector which might tie in with some of our earlier thinking about what motivates people to go to work. This reading is also intended to introduce the idea that many different aspects of HRM will be needed to ensure that we get the right people with the right skills to deal with the often multi-faceted roles within the retailing sector.

The job of a chocolate taster:

So you want to work in …

Confectionery

For the sweet-toothed, a job in confectionery – particularly in product-tasting – will be a mouth-watering career option. Who wouldn't want to spend their days munching on chocolate bars in the line of duty? A dream job like this will, undoubtedly, have its downside – the cost of new trousers when all that eating starts to tell on your waistline, for one thing – but it's hard to find too many. There is a variety of jobs in this field, from the scientific side of product development to marketing and getting products on to the shelves. But most of these will probably include a spot of tasting, so it's wise to get a job working on a product you like.

An employer says …

Mark Sims, graduate recruitment manager, Waitrose (waitrose.com)

Many people become buyers, working in a category of food such as confectionery, after working in a store or other retail departments such as in supply chain at head office. It's important for buyers to have some experience in a branch or in retail so they have a greater understanding of how the business works. It's likely that "partners" (as all Waitrose employees are known) will have various roles throughout the business before moving to become a buyer.

We have four graduate schemes in the John Lewis Partnership – two in retail management, one in John Lewis and one in Waitrose. These two schemes give a grounding in managing a large team of people in a high-pressure environment, plus commercial experience.

Being a buyer involves the ability to see the wider picture as well as having good analytical skills. You will manage a category of food rather than a team of people. You could find yourself travelling overseas finding inspiration for new product lines, as well as liaising with suppliers and monitoring the production process all the way from the initial idea to seeing the end product on the shelves. It's very rewarding to see a product you have championed flying off the shelves of a Waitrose branch.

An academic says ...

Dr Richard Frazier, head of food and bioprocessing sciences group, University of Reading (reading.ac.uk)

There are many exciting challenges facing the food industry and there is a constant demand for food science and food technology graduates who possess a strong scientific and technical skill base, combined with an understanding of how to manage consumer issues concerning food safety, quality and nutrition. Graduate careers are among the most rewarding among professional groups in terms of salary and promotion prospects. Recent graduates from Reading have gained employment in all areas of the food industry.

We train our graduates in sensory science, which involves designing, performing and evaluating results of sensory panels. This is a key aspect of food quality.

Generally speaking, food production companies set up taste panels to monitor the quality of products leaving the factory. This would consist of staff who have been trained to look for certain attributes of the product, and could mean tasting a wide range of products. It is rare that someone would focus on one particular food type or work individually. Taste panels are trained in the specific sensory properties of a food, such as mouth feel, texture and flavour.

There is a shortage of food science and food technology graduates leaving UK universities and our graduates can command above-average starting salaries of about £25,000 plus benefits.

A graduate says ...

Gervase Fay, product developer, confectionery department, Sainsbury's (sainsburys.co.uk)

I've been at Sainsbury's for a year, and in my current role for two months. My job is to develop confectionery products at fair prices for customers. We look at customer needs and market location, and we go out and get inspiration, develop packaging and design and get the product delivered into stores. I'm involved in all that.

We constantly sample products to check they meet our standards. Every week we have a sampling session to check all the products meet the Sainsbury's checklist.

I did a degree in retail and my role is to work within the customer department, understanding their needs as well as marketing the product. We have food technicians, who need to have a food science degree, who deal with the technical aspects.

What we look for is the right packaging and if the product tastes nice. When we taste the product we look out for the flavours – what it's like to eat, how it feels in the mouth, to bite.

I love sampling chocolate – I could do it every day. At the moment, I'm happy to keep learning, but in the future I would like to own a small food store. I don't know what I'll sell, perhaps chocolate.

I've just finished working on ensuring all our products have no added flavours and colours, which was a big project for us. I'm now concentrating on Easter. Christmas has been and gone for us. It was strange celebrating Christmas in July.

Source: Guardian 25/10/2008

A serious point from this article about a particular career in the retail sector is the variety of roles one could play within a job. As a store manager, your responsibility would be to try and fit the right person to that job and/or those roles and to help the people feel responsibility for fulfilling the role, to feel motivated and to help them to develop the skills to be able to perform and progress within it. On this note, the next activity asks you to reflect on possible career paths in retailing.

 Activity 3.1 Working in retailing (TGF)

Spend about 15 minutes this activity

Purpose: to consider possible implications of working at different levels in a retail organisation.

Task: Study figure 3.1 and reflect on how job roles vary depending on where an individual works in the organisation.

Feedback

At an operational level the focus of job roles is on day-to-day operations and tactical business issues. At the head office level, the focus is strategic and job roles are associated with longer-term activities. The specialised functions focus on particular areas which both facilitate strategic planning and at the same time ensure operational effectiveness.

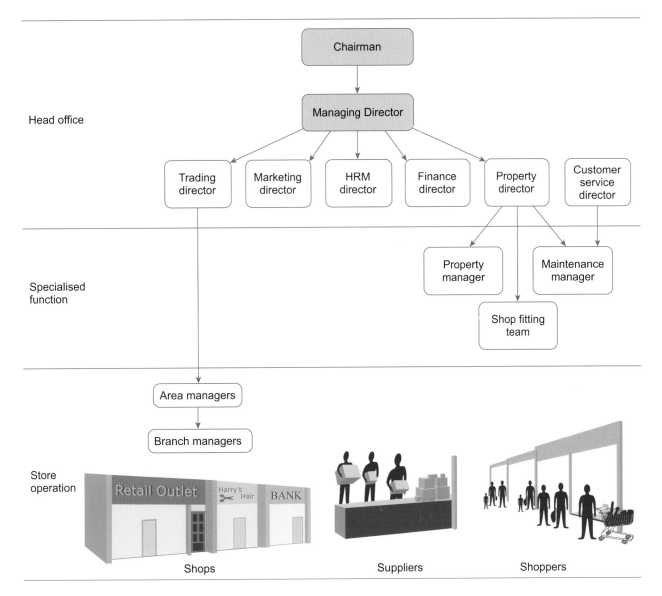

Figure 3.1 Different levels in retail organisations

In the following sections we will look in more detail at some HRM activities.

3.2 Selection and recruitment

In HRM terms, selection refers to the processes involved in choosing the most suitable applicant for a given post. The selection process is sometimes considered purely from the manager's viewpoint, although it is likely that other members of existing staff will have an input into the process.

A building society is a financial services institution owned by its members.

According to a study by Purcell and Kinnie (2007), selection processes were particularly important in the case of the Nationwide Building Society, (a retail financial service organisation in the UK).

At the time of this research, the Nationwide Building Society was the UK's largest retail financial services organisation, providing its members with a wide range of financial service products. Of its 16,500 staff, around half were employed in branches around the UK and over 80 per cent were women. A detailed demographic breakdown of this staff suggests that only a small minority of the women employed were over 50 (8 per cent of the

reported sample) and only 6 per cent of Nationwide employees were drawn from the minority ethnic sections of the community.

Given the importance of customer service skills, the Nationwide needs to ensure that HRM selects and recruits the right employees. A central tool in the recruitment and selection process is the job description that lays out the tasks and activities the successful applicant will be expected to be able to perform competently. An accompanying document, the person specification, describes the attributes required of the potential job holder. These are often divided into 'essential' and 'desirable' skills so applicants can be evaluated fairly. It is useful for both the employer and potential employee to have a clear idea of what the job involves and what skills will be needed now and in the future to perform the role successfully.

There are a number of stages which can be used to define and set out the nature of particular jobs for recruitment purposes:

- Job analysis is the process of examining jobs in order to identify the key requirements of each job.

- A job description sets out how a particular employee will fit into the organisation. It could be used as a job indicator for applicants for a job or as a guideline for an employee and/or their line manager as to their roles and responsibilities in the organisation.

- A job specification highlights the mental and physical attributes required of the job holder. For example, for a trainee manager's post in a retail store it might include the following (taken from a real advertisement):

  > Managers at all levels would be expected to show responsibility. The company is looking for people who are tough and talented. They should have a flair for business; know how to sell and work in a team.

The processes of job analysis and compiling a job description and person specification can all provide useful information to a business, in addition to serving as recruitment instruments. Job details can serve as a useful basis for establishing communications and setting targets with employees. Job descriptions can also be used as reference points for arbitrating in disputes as to 'who does what' in a business.

Sometimes, rather than looking outside an organisation to fill a job vacancy, it may be advantageous to look inside the organisation. In addition to cost savings, it may be that a promotion or secondment would enhance employee motivation. Let's look at this idea more closely in the following activity.

Activity 3.2 Internal vs. external recruitment

Spend about 20 minutes on this activity.

Purpose: to consider the advantages and disadvantages of internal and external approaches to recruitment.

Task: Read the extract in Box 3.1. When you have considered the main ideas, imagine that you are in a position where you need to make a case to your line manager for recruiting a new member of staff using either an internal or external recruitment approach.

Box 3.1 Recruitment, selection and training

Recruiting individuals to fill particular posts in a business can be done either internally, from within the business, or externally by recruiting people from outside.

Internal recruitment

The advantages of internal recruitment are that:

Induction and socialisation are aspects of HRM theory which explore the ways in which employees start to understand the formal and informal structures and cultures that exist in an organisation.

1 Considerable savings can be made. Individuals with inside knowledge of how a business operates may need shorter periods of training and time for 'fitting in' or induction and socialisation.
2 The organisation is unlikely to be disrupted greatly by someone who is used to working with others in the organisation.
3 Internal promotion acts as an incentive to all staff to work harder within the organisation.
4 From the firm's point of view, the strengths and weaknesses of an insider will have been assessed. There is always a risk attached to employing an outsider who may be a success 'on paper' only.

The disadvantages of recruiting from within are that:

1 The manager may have to recruit to fill the position vacated by the person who has been promoted.
2 An insider may be less likely to make the essential criticisms required to get the company working more effectively.
3 Promotion of one person in a company may upset someone else.

External recruitment

The advantages of external recruitment are that it:

1 makes it possible to draw on a wider range of talent
2 provides the opportunity to bring new experience and ideas into the business.

The disadvantages of external recruitment are that:

1 it is more costly
2 the company may end up with someone who proves less effective in practice than they appeared to be on paper and at the interview.

Feedback

Whichever approach you have chosen (internal or external recruitment) might have been affected by your own experience or that of others you know at work. If you were preparing a report on either you may want to mention the following:

Case for internal recruitment:

Internal recruitment offers the advantage of cost savings and the recruitment of individuals who are already known to the organisation. Their level of performance, commitment, and motivation should also be known. The internal recruit already knows how the company works in terms of procedures and protocols, which can reduce the need for training. This individual is also likely to have built an internal social network and connections which enable them to function effectively within the organisation.

Case for external recruitment:

External recruitment offers the advantage of gaining new skills and selecting an individual who fits the job role. The external person can bring fresh ideas and competencies to the company. Drawing from a wider pool of potential recruits can result in better qualified and more able individuals being attracted to the job vacancy.

If you were to draw on actual examples in your report, it may make it more convincing. How would individuals in a retail store, for example, feel about a new employee recruited internally or externally? What types of retail stores would tend to take which approach do you think? This may be an interesting discussion point for your tutor group forum.

3.3 Training and development

Individuals recruited to a post may not have all the skills needed to do the job. This is the role of training and development within the HRM function. As we noted earlier, many roles within retailing involve a myriad of responsibilities and the skills to perform them. Taking the buying function within a retail business as an example, here is a list of some of the tasks performed by people in this function:

- long-term strategic planning
- market analysis
- identifying new markets
- identifying and selecting products

The Argos catalogue store, where flat-panel television screens are used to monitor order progress

- product design and product specification
- new product launches, promotions, and marketing events
- stock control and availability
- stock levels in stores
- selecting, negotiating and monitoring suppliers
- sales forecasting and performance monitoring
- budgeting and finance
- sales promotions and sales events (controlling prices).

Within the buying function, jobs are designed to focus on a proportion of these tasks rather than the whole list. It is important to note that in a small organisation the buyer will be responsible for a wider set of tasks.

You will learn more about the buying function in Block 4.

Training enables staff to put their skills and abilities to the best possible use within a retail organisation. If an organisation offers good levels of training, staff are likely to be better able to perform their job's roles and responsibilities – and good training schemes can help retain staff. Ideally, all staff will have opportunity to review and enhance their skills throughout their employment.

Identifying training needs

The education and training of needs of individual employees will vary according to which stage they are at. Cox and Brittain (2003, p. 238) suggest there are four broad classes of training in the retail sector:

1 **New entrants** need to learn about the business and should be invited to follow an induction programme soon after joining. The induction should provide essential information about the business and its operational procedures, including health, safety and security. Additionally, new

starters will need training in customer relations, product knowledge, how to sell, how internal systems and specific technology work (e.g., checkouts), cash handling and accounting for daily sales.

2 **Established staff** require occasional retraining as well as introductions to new techniques and procedures. It is important to assess the training needs of established staff to ensure appropriate training is offered.

3 **Selected staff** are individuals whose skills the retailer wishes to develop. Most retailers have management training schemes to help suitable individuals move through the business into jobs with additional responsibilities. Skillsmart Retail is a Government agency which works with retailers to identify the skills required in retailing. Indeed, studying this module fits into the national framework and has put you on a retail career pathway (should that be of interest to you).

4 **Management** needs training programmes that are going to add value by enabling the business to run more efficiently and for managers to develop to their full capacity; developing the future senior managers and the workforce. Management training in retailing covers specific specialist areas such as finance, merchandising, HRM and property management.

Cox and Brittain suggest that each class of training has different requirements and it is important to develop suitable and appropriate training at each level. Let's explore this further in the following activity.

Activity 3.3 Designing training programmes

Spend about 30 minutes on this activity.

Purpose: to identify different approaches to training development.

Task: Now read about how Danish grocery retailers design training programmes for different types of retail employees and consider the wider implications of this study for retail training and development.

Box 3.2 Training in Danish grocery retail

A study of the checkout operators and front-line sales employees in five Danish grocery retail chains found that training and development programmes for their retail stores were targeted at different employees. The employees were chosen for training because of the differences managers perceived between their motivations and ambitions and those of other employees (Esbjerg et al., 2010). These researchers found that one category of employee, which they described as 'career seeker', was more likely to receive training and development than other store staff. Esbjerg et al. categorised other staff as either 'transition workers' or 'core employees'. These three different groups of employees are described in more detail below:

- **Transition workers** – people who did not necessarily plan to stay in retail, but were working in the sector for a short period doing part-time work, (students, for example).
- **Core employees** – people, often with many years of retailing experience, who tended to be older than the transitional workers and

yet who expressed no ambition or desire to move into a management position. These people were considered good and stable workers and were used to train others.

- **Career seekers** – people who had moved into the retailing sector to forge a career, perhaps due to a widely believed impression, in Denmark as elsewhere, that it is possible to achieve a management position in the retailing industry relatively quickly and without formal management qualifications.

In this research, the training and development programmes of career seekers were practically orientated and focused on skills training of immediate relevance to the workplace. For example, the researchers noted that managers were trained in how to conduct recruitment interviews, whereas transitional workers and core employees received only basic 'on-the-job' training.

(Esbjerg et al., 2010)

Feedback

Whether a retailer chooses to develop training around specific tasks and procedures or skills and motivations there are some basic considerations. Possibly the most important is to determine who is responsible for organising and managing training and development. In small retail organisations, this is likely to be a director but in larger organisations, say those with over 500 employees, there is likely to be a training and development officer. Throughout the workforce there should be job descriptions, which set out the tasks for each job role and these should help to analyse individual training needs. In order to implement an efficient training programme across the workforce, it is important to be able to measure performance and this is usually done by the process of appraisal.

We can see how an appraisal system might be linked to training and rewards in the next section.

3.4 Appraisal and rewards

A performance appraisal, often conducted on an annual basis (but preferably more often), is a means of documenting an agreement between an employee and a line manager about what the manager expects of the employee over the appraisal period. Sometimes this may also include discussion of personal development needs and pay and benefits (or rewards) such as holiday entitlements, bonuses and premium payments, company sick pay and pensions.

Rewards may be split into two categories: extrinsic rewards and intrinsic rewards. Extrinsic rewards are related to pay and benefits in return for work efforts. Intrinsic rewards are an individual's positive feelings as a direct result of doing satisfying work. Individual employees may well have different opinions about the importance of the balance between extrinsic and intrinsic rewards. Reward systems may be designed to ensure that individual motivational needs are met successfully; see our earlier exploration of theories about individual motivation at work. We can see this in the following example.

Performance-related pay (PRP) is one way of relating rewards directly to an assessment of individual performance. This is where workers receive extra pay or benefits directly related to meeting targets or for working beyond expectations. There is some debate whether this is motivational to staff or not; sometimes it is seen as divisive, particularly if the criteria set for PRP and who receives it is not transparent.

Retail concessions are found in many retail locations (e.g., airports, train stations and department stores). In a department store, some of the goods are 'own-bought' and the retail concession (usually a brand) provides stock and, sometimes, the staff to run the concession in return for commission on sales (goods sold within the store).

In a study of changing HRM practices at Selfridges (a leading London department store on Oxford Street), Purcell and Kinnie (2007) examined employee attitudes to performance-related pay (PRP) and the staff discount. The company had, at that time, recently reviewed its HRM practices to promote its new, upmarket, innovative and vibrant 'store for the next century' brand. The staff surveyed included both those employed directly by the store, and additional staff who worked in a variety of concessionary retail outlets.

On the one hand, the study showed positive correlation between performance-related pay for both store and concessionary employees' levels of commitment and job autonomy. On the other hand, the most significant factor in determining whether employees' attitudes were positive or negative was individuals' perceptions of the leadership behaviours of their first-line managers.

 Retail sectors ————————————————————

Motivation, communication and performance appraisals in the UK charity sector.

Parsons and Broadbridge (2006) studied the UK charity sector and identified four issues that caused dissatisfaction among managers of charity shops:

1 poor working conditions

2 low salary levels

3 organisational climate

4 communication.

Their research suggests that issues 1 and 2 relate to the nature of this particular type of retail store work which involves long hours and monotonous, labour-intensive tasks.

Factors 3 and 4 are more likely to be caused by poor in-store relations and a lack of head office support. This study focuses on management communications in the charity sector and discovers that communication is one of the main means by which to motivate retail store employees.

You may think that it is unusual to look at the charity shop sector, as there are fewer than 10,000 charity store workers in the United Kingdom. However, charity shop managers have many challenging responsibilities to deal with, which go beyond the general retail management practices in a typical for-profit high-street store. For example, charity shops sell products randomly donated by members of the public; this means there is no continuity of supply or guarantee of quality. Another significant issue is the management of a workforce that usually consists of paid employees and unpaid volunteers, which can be a highly volatile mix that results in conflict between the two groups of workers. Broadbridge and Parsons (2003) showed that charity shop managers require sophisticated people skills in addition to the specialist skills of retail managers and entrepreneurs. Therefore, by considering the charity sector, we can explore the breadth of skills required to manage a workforce in general and in more complex and challenging circumstances.

Broadbridge and Parsons, (2003) found there has been a notable increase in the number of paid managers and staff in stores, which previously were roles staffed by volunteers. As charities have become more professional, operating expenditure has risen. Indeed, Parsons, (2002, p. 587), states:

> … expenditure on wages having the most significant impact on profits. Shops that were traditionally run solely on volunteer effort now employ at least one paid manager and those that previously employed a single manager now employ two to stay abreast of the competition. In fact, there have been changes to the whole mode and ethos of managing the shops.

Furthermore, many retail managers have left privately owned companies to join charity organisations; their previous retail store experience affected wider organisational management causing a shift from decentralised, local control to more centralised methods of management, which creates opportunities to introduce more head office support, monitoring and control methods. As a result, there has been an increase in the attention paid to formalised human resource management practices in the charity sector, including the use of more formal appraisal systems as a way of understanding, communicating and subsequently motivating store managers and the wider workforce.

Broadly speaking, an appraisal system is a process devised to assess employees' performance against selected criteria, which may include, job satisfaction, personal development and work-related performance. However, according to Payne et al. (2009), the most important consideration when conducting appraisals is to evaluate 'employees on relevant behaviours that are aligned to the overall organisational mission and doing so in a fair and equitable manner.' In other words, an effective appraisal system is one that employees see as useful, effective, and fair, which increases the need for the charity shop manager to be sensitive to these differences between paid and unpaid staff when carrying out appraisals.

Activity 3.4 Formal appraisal systems

Spend about 20 minutes on this activity.

Purpose: to identify potential advantages and disadvantages associated with implementing an appraisal system in the charity sector.

Task: Imagine you are the manager of a charity store in your local area who is considering the introduction of a formal appraisal system of the paid and unpaid staff who work in the store. Suggest the possible advantages and disadvantages for:

1   the paid and unpaid staff

2   the managers at your head office

3   you, as the local store manager.

Feedback

1 The paid and unpaid staff

Advantages:

An appraisal system might enable your staff to discuss with you as the manager any difficulties or problems they have about their work. An appraisal also creates an opportunity to discover what aspects of the job motivate individuals and can identify dissatisfiers, particularly among the unpaid staff.

Disadvantages:

There might be differences in how volunteers and paid employees view the introduction of a formal appraisal system. There could be resistance, especially among unpaid staff, who might feel inclined to challenge the usefulness of such a system.

2 The managers at your head office

Advantages:

An appraisal system gives head office managers a means to communicate business objectives to the local staff. It also provides a way of capturing whether or not these objectives are reflected in individual goals, often agreed as part of a formal appraisal system process.

Formal appraisal systems provide a means of monitoring the performance of local store managers, highlighting levels of motivation between different types of staff and creating opportunities to develop effective training and staff development programmes.

Disadvantages:

Difficulties associated with assessing volunteer and paid staff on an equal basis could arise.

Costs are associated with developing and implementing different appraisal systems to meet the needs of different types of staff. Conflict and tension could result from a poorly implemented system.

3 You, as the local store manager

Advantages and disadvantages:

For you, as the manager of a local charity store, a formal appraisal system might seem something of a mixed blessing. Even effectively designed appraisal systems generate an additional administration burden. You might already have good interpersonal relationships with the staff and not feel the need for a formal system. Alternatively, you might welcome the system as a means to develop staff and to improve the performance of the charity shop, believing that an appraisal system might open up another local channel of communication through which employees' ideas and comments could flow.

The points above are not intended as a definitive answer to the question of whether formal appraisal systems are a 'good' idea or not but to encourage you to think about the different viewpoints that need to be considered when implementing an appraisal system.

 End of theme

3.5 Conclusions

In this study session we have looked at some HRM practices in retail store management such as recruitment, training and appraisals. In the final section, we considered the advantages and disadvantages of appraisal systems in a specific retail sector: the not-for-profit voluntary sector. In the next study session, we will look in more detail at how and why 'customer service' seems to have become an increasingly important in retailing.

Learning outcomes

When you have completed all the study elements for this session, you should be able to:

- identify and explain some significant elements of the HRM function
- discuss how the HRM function contributes to retail operations
- develop your problem-solving skills in an HRM context
- reflect on your own ideas and work with others as part of your tutor group forum.

Session 4 Managing customers

A retail store is a place where shoppers go to browse, select and purchase a myriad of goods and services but it also creates the environment in which retailers deliver customer service and this experience can be excellent, poor or somewhere inbetween. In this session, we explore customer service management, beginning with the customer, and then working through the services a retailer might offer and the levels of service they might provide. The ability to evaluate and explain why a retailer has adopted a given approach to customer service is an important academic skill and you will be expected to demonstrate this capacity in the tutor-marked assignment (TMA) that accompanies this block.

First, let's consider the customer and see why individuals go shopping and what informs the way they behave.

4.1 Shoppers' motivations and missions

Why do we choose to spend our time there? A busy shopping street scene

From a retailer's perspective, it is important to understand the average consumer's behaviour during a shopping trip in order to design the retail store appropriately. As we have already learnt, retailers select formats and locations that will enable them to meet customers' needs. But we are now thinking about a new level of complexity for the retailer to consider: the shopper's underlying mission for going shopping and the attitude and motivations of the shopper.

For many years, retailing academics have tried to categorise individual shoppers by the way that they shop. Tauber (1972, cited in Varley and Rafiq, 2004), one of the first researchers to investigate this area, appreciated that there were reasons for shopping other than the simple necessity to purchase physical products. He found that consumers' behaviour in a retail setting are derived from many factors, some of which are less related to the buying of products and more related to individuals' personal and social motivations. He went on to suggest that, if retailers are to fully understand consumers' motivations for shopping, they need to consider the satisfaction that a consumer gets from the shopping activity itself, as well as the benefits obtained from the product(s) bought.

Activity 4.1 Shopping motivations

Spend about 20 minutes on this activity

Purpose: to consider shopping motivations

Task: Study images A–D

Image A: H&M, central Copenhagen, midday sunny Saturday, Image B: Sainsbury's supermarket, London Colney, Image C: Grafton Street Dublin, Ireland, weekday afternoon, Image D: Arty Crafty, independent retailer in Boughton-on-the-Water in the Cotswolds on a sunny Sunday afternoon

Now complete Table 4.1 by adding what you think is motivating the individuals to be in the particular shopping environment. This is quite a complex activity, you should look at the individuals, their body language and the retail setting for clues to possible motivations. You might find it helps to imagine you are in each location and try to think what would motivate you to be in each location. Select your answers from Varley & Rafiq's list of shopper motivations.

According to Varley & Rafiq, (2004, p. 66), the motivations for going shopping are:

Self-reward: The need to treat oneself or put yourself in a positive frame of mind by buying something you like.

Exercise: the need to get out and about and get some fresh air.

Personal stimulation: the need for an experience, enjoyment of being in an interesting and/or different environment.

Learning: the need to acquire new knowledge in order to become an 'educated shopper'; finding out about new products, following fashion trends, talking to experts in stores.

Role-play: the need to reinforce a role or to play a role to which one aspires; for example the role of the provider (gathering the family's weekly needs).

Diversion: the need to alleviate boredom.

Social experiences: the need to be with friends, to talk to others with similar interests and to have contact with peer group.

Status and power: the need to exert authority, to gain attention from retail personnel, to have somebody serve and show respect.

Bargain hunting: the need to show expertise in finding value in purchasing; the need to have 'beaten' the retailer by buying at discounted prices.

Table 4.1 (a) Shopper motivations

Image	Suggest shopper motivations
Image A: H&M, central Copenhagen, midday sunny Saturday	
Image B: Sainsbury's supermarket, London Colney	
Image C: Grafton Street Dublin, Ireland, weekday afternoon	
Image D: Arty Crafty, independent retailer in Boughton-on-the-Water in the Cotswolds on a sunny Sunday afternoon	

Feedback

This is a difficult exercise but you have been given some clues to help you think about the motivations of the shoppers in each of these situations.

Table 4.1 (b) Shopper motivations

Image	Suggest shopper motivations
Image A: H&M	Personal stimulation – the need for an experience, enjoyment of being in an interesting and/or different environment.
Image B: Sainsbury's supermarket	Role-play – the need to reinforce a role or play a role to which one aspires; for example the role of the provider (gathering the family's weekly needs).
Image C: Grafton Street Dublin	Exercise – the need to get out and about and get some fresh air. Or Diversion – the need to alleviate boredom, to break routine and get out and about.
Image D: Arty Crafty	Social experiences – the need to be with friends, to talk to others with similar interests and to have contact with peer group.

Shopping missions

Levels of involvement in purchasing affect: how we come to a purchase decision; the number of criteria we use to make the selection; and the amount of time we take to make the purchase decision. You will explore these ideas in more detail in Block 3.

You might be thinking, 'how does the underlying motivation to go shopping link to the type of shopping we might do once in the retail environment and what are the implications for retail managers?' From the retailers' point of view one of the key differences between types of shopping trips is that for chore or low-involvement shopping, it is in the shoppers' interest to establish a routine so that the shopping trip can be carried out as efficiently as possible. One of the ways shoppers might do this is to always go to the same store, and perhaps to choose a store which enables them to buy as many of the things that they normally need as quickly as possible. You may have found that, once you are familiar with the store layout, you can shop more quickly – and for me it then becomes frustrating when the retailer moves products around. However, when I buy a high-involvement product, I am much more likely to shop around and to consider carefully several alternative products from different retail providers.

These differences suggest that the way in which we shop may be influenced by our shopping mission. Varley and Rafiq (2004, p. 65) illustrate this idea using the following accounts of shopping for a product which they describe as 'square sheets of absorbent paper'. They suggest that although the product in each instance is similar, the reasons we as shoppers may want to buy it, vary – and retailers may be able, therefore, to alter the ways in which they present their products in order to meet our differing needs.

Box 4.1: Square sheets of absorbent paper

- **Emergency situation** – Suffering from hay fever, Alice is in need of a packet of tissues fast! She will buy them from the nearest outlet that has product available. Product attributes such as price, brand, quality and design are not so relevant to her in this situation. Convenience stores may therefore be able to apply a higher profit margin to this type of product in these shopping circumstances.

- **Routine buying** – On a visit to a supermarket to do the weekly household shop, Dipak purchases a family pack of tissues. He assumes the current pack at home will not last much longer. He may be influenced by promotional offers (such as 2 for 1) and may use other product criteria such as colour and use of recycled materials in his purchase decision making. Although his overall involvement in the purchase is likely to be low, he may expect the tissues to be competitively priced.

- **Destination shopping** – Chris is organising a dinner party. She needs to buy some table napkins and she is concerned that the quality of the napkins reflects her excellent cookery skills and that the design complements the décor in her dining room. She heads for a department store in a nearby regional shopping centre where she knows she will find a wide selection of designs from which to choose. She is not price-sensitive in her purchase, although she believes this reputable retailer provides good value for money. She is most concerned about selecting the right 'look'.

- **Browsing** – Jack is doing his Christmas shopping. Whilst browsing through a variety store he notices some novelty tissues with cartoon characters printed on them. He decides that these could make a good stocking-filler present for his 9-year-old daughter. He then moves into the male toiletries section to find an equivalent gift for his 11-year-old son.

(Adapted from Varley and Rafiq, 2004, p. 65)

So far, we have explored how shopping motivations and missions might influence where, why and when we shop. In the next section, we are going to look deeper into the shoppers' psyche and find out about types of shoppers.

Types of shoppers

Alterations in shoppers' behaviours in relation to 'shopping missions' and the services that they wish to receive are of interest to retailers – as they may mean that current retail service levels need to be rethought. One piece of research investigated the relationship between shoppers' motivations and retail store formats. Ganesh et al. (2007) identify five different shopper 'types' as follows:

- **Apathetic** – these shoppers are described as 'indifferent towards shopping' (Ganesh et al., 2007, p. 378). Apathetic shoppers lack a strong motivation to shop and aim to complete their shopping 'missions' as effectively and efficiently as possible.

- **Enthusiasts** – these are the people who really enjoy shopping, which they see as a means of entertainment.

- **Destination** – destination shoppers are motivated primarily by the desire to obtain new and fashionable products. Mall and other branded retail outlets are these shoppers' retail destinations of choice based on the shops' image and the shoppers' desire to seek out newness.

- **Basic** – basic shoppers don't appear to gain strong satisfaction from shopping. They are clear about the products and services that they wish to purchase, go directly to the most convenient store, and aim simply to select and purchase products in the least possible amount of time. These people view shopping as a necessary function rather than a recreational activity.

- **Bargain seekers** – the final category of shoppers that Ganesh et al. identified was that of 'bargain seekers'. These shoppers are motivated primarily by price reductions and, to a lesser extent, shop for goods and services which meet their individual needs. No other aspects of the shopping experience seem to interest them.

This is a useful illustration of shopper types and it is helpful for retail managers to consider who their shoppers are in order to identify which products to sell, how to display the products, communicate with the customers and determine the levels of service to offer. Please note this is not the only classification of types of shoppers, but it is important because it illustrates the principle of sorting shoppers into meaningful groups that have implications for retailers. Many retailers invest in market research to identify shopper types and this forms the basis of their target marketing strategy. We will cover these ideas in detail in Block 3. For the time being we are interested in the notion of different shopper types and the implications for customer service management.

4.2 Retail services

Retailers provide goods and services for sale to a whole range of customer types. Some retailers sell pure goods and others pure services but many offer a range of physical products and additional wrap-around services such as delivery, credit facilities, installation and after-sales support. The range and type of additional services are a management decision, and part of the way a retailer creates advantage over their competitors.

Once a retailer has identified which additional services to provide, they must decide on the level of service to offer and this is an important linkage to shopping missions and shopper types.

The extent and range of additional services offered by retailers vary. In Box 4.2 the various types of additional services are outlined.

Box 4.2 Additional services

Product-related services

These are add-on services to a product and they vary according to the type of product, for example:

- A fashion retailer might provide changing rooms to try clothing, alteration services, a personal shopper to help with the selection of clothing and a returns policy for faulty items.

- A retailer of white goods (refrigerators, washing machines, etc.) might provide product selection guides and technical advice, installation services, after-sales service support, guarantees and product insurance.

- A furniture retailer might provide delivery services, layout and room design services, fitting and aftercare advice and support.

As additional services are increasingly used competitively to differentiate retailers from one another, service offerings are becoming more complex. Retailers are even offering custom-made packages to suit the need of particular types of shoppers.

Convenience-related services

As consumers have less and less time to shop, retailers have responded by putting together packages that aim to make the shopping experience as convenient as possible. Grocery retailers have been particularly proactive in this area and you might expect the following add-on services when you visit a large supermarket, superstore or hypermarket:

- help with packing
- home delivery
- restaurant and cafe facilities
- children's crèche
- toilets
- extended opening hours
- cash machines
- supermarket trolleys with different sizes and functions, for example, trolleys that include child seats
- segregated car parking, giving easier access to the disabled and parents with children.

Additionally, grocery retailers provide services that enhance the convenience of visiting the store and aim to encourage shoppers to do all of their shopping there rather than visiting speciality stores. Many supermarkets provide services such as an in-store pharmacy, bakery, delicatessen, dry-cleaners, and photographic processing services.

As retailers have found, add-on services are a very effective way to improve convenience, enhance the customers' shopping experience and strategically improve market share. There is an ongoing competitive battle in the supermarket sector to provide the best all-round service.

Payment services

In order to provide a high level of convenience in the shopping process, retailers offer a range of payment services in order to avoid any barriers resulting from a customer's preferred payment method being unavailable. Typical payment methods used in retailing include: cash, debit card, credit card, store account card, hire purchase (often with payment protection insurance), and monthly payments by direct debit (with additional guarantees).

It is important to note that payment arrangements allow a customer to complete a purchase and provide an opportunity for retailers to build relationships through data collection.

Product availability

If a retailer is out of stock of a particular item, the customer will be disappointed and may go elsewhere. This situation is a failure on the retailers' part, and savvy retailers use this as a opportunity to create a service recovery situation by delivering out-of-stock products direct to the customer's home.

Information services

Retailers provide information about products via call centres as well as in-store (as you learnt in the podcasts and associated activities in Multimedia activities 2). Product knowledge and information aids the purchasing process and can be provided in various ways, for example; in person, by telephone, online or in print.

Customer sales service

Contact between the customer and sales staff is most apparent in a retail store. The interaction between these parties can be passive or highly interactive.

(Source: based on Varley and Rafiq, 2003)

 ## Activity 4.2 Retail formats and levels of customer service

Spend about 15 minutes on this activity.

Purpose: to consider the relationship between the format and levels of customer service.

Task: Look at Table 4.2 which shows retail format and customer sales service.

Table 4.2 Retail format and customer sales service

Retail format	Staffing levels	Need for product knowledge and experience	Profit margins
Supermarket	Medium	Low	Low
Speciality store	High	High	High
Department store	High	High	High
Category killer	Low	High	Low
Discount store	Low	Low	Low
Non-store	Medium-low	Medium-low	Low

(Varley and Rafiq, 2003, p. 255)

Now answer these questions:

1   Which is the strongest predictor of the level of service provided in a particular format?

2   Suggest why it is important to consider staffing levels for different retail formats.

Feedback

Levels of customer sales service are closely linked to retailer profit margins and pricing strategy.

The level of service must be appropriate for the products being sold and meet the expectations of the target customers. Therefore, in a discount supermarket such as Lidl or Aldi, expectations are low in terms of level of availability of customer sales staff and product knowledge whereas in a department store (such as Debenhams, John Lewis Partnership, or Harrods) expectations are reversed.

What are service encounters?

According to Ford (2001) it is useful to make a distinction between types of service interactions. She describes these as service encounters, service relationships and personalised service.

- **Service encounters** are a single interaction between a customer and a service provider, which in our case is the retailer. From a retailer's point of view, service encounters need to achieve maximum efficiency and transactions are designed to enable as many customers as possible to be processed. This means interactions between the retail store staff and their customers are likely to be as short as possible. From the worker's point of view, that can mean their job is repetitive, monotonous and routine. For instance, the retailer may tell their employees to 'be friendly', to smile, and to use scripted phrases to open and close customer interactions. Employees receive standardised training and need use only this knowledge to do the job. Service encounters of this type are found typically in fast-food restaurants. Not all retail service encounters are so straightforward – retail banking frontline staff process a range of more complicated tasks.

- **Service relationships** occur when there is repeated contact between a customer and a particular service provider. Transactions are likely to take longer, particularly in the initial stages of a relationship.

  Appointments may be scheduled between the customer and the provider (e.g., a kitchen designer). The provider is expected to share information with the customer, for example the range of options from which the customer may choose. Such retail service work is flexible and dynamic.

  A wide range of tasks is performed and performance is altered to tailor the service to each customer. In some cases the customer and the provider may develop a real friendship. Providers are typically well-paid professionals with specialised expertise.

- **Personalised services** are tailored to the unique needs of each individual customer, for example in an expensive department store where you choose your clothes with the help of a personal shopper. Ford (2001 p. 4) found four aspects that differentiate personalised service:

  - Customer orientation: this means that employees who offer personalised services engage in 'communication behaviours that enable them to identify a customer's specific needs and tailor their service to meet those needs'.

  - Interaction involvement: employees show that they are interested and engaged in the interaction by their attentiveness, signalled through non-verbal gestures such as nodding, eye contact and leaning forward. They will be perceptive in their interpretation of customers' needs.

  - Information sharing: appropriate means will be deployed to share information with the customer. At a minimum, this means allocating sufficient time to give the customers the information that they need, particularly if their purchase is a new and important item. The customer may also need to feel they have made an informed decision or to see how the product or service addresses directly a particular concern. Information needs to be deliberately given in a language the customers understand, avoiding the use of, or need for, technical terms wherever possible.

  - Social support: this means that employees help customers to meet the personal demands of a situation. This may be directive guidance; making the interaction fun or more relaxed; showing interest in the customers' well-being, feelings and needs; or the provision of practical help, perhaps in the form of transportation or a referral to another service provider.

Ford found that customer expectations of service encounters and service relations differed significantly. For example, whilst customers expected social interactions with all service interactions, in service encounters anything more time-consuming than a friendly approach was considered a disadvantage. In service relationships, however, customers expected service providers to spend more time with them and to engage in social conversations.

It is important for retailers to know the level of service they aim to deliver. In Block 1 we examined service products and considered that delivering a service is akin to performance. Can you remember? We identified how gaps could appear between the service offered by a retailer and the expectations of the customers.

The four 'gaps' identified by Parasuraman et al. (1985 and 1990) are:

- the consumer expectation – management perception gap (Gap 1)
- the management perception – service quality specification gap (Gap 2)
- the service quality specification – service delivery gap (Gap 3)
- the service delivery – external communications gap (Gap 4).

Now we can consider the model developed by Parasuraman et al (Figure 4.1), in further detail. Look at Figure 4.1 the service quality model and think about what the model means for retail managers responsible for managing customer service.

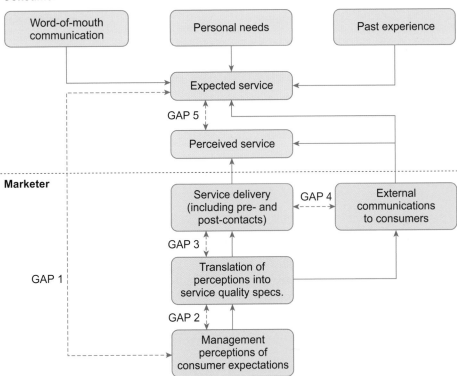

Figure 4.1 Parasuraman et al.'s (1985) service quality model (Source: Parasuraman et al., 1985, p. 50)

Managers face the following difficulties at each of the potential gaps:

Gap 1 relates to the difficulties managers may have in understanding in advance what features of their service are of particular importance to consumers.

Gap 2 relates to the difficulties managers experience trying to match or indeed exceed consumers' expectations.

Gap 3 describes the uncertainty related to service performance, even when there are clear guidelines about how to perform the service well and about how to treat consumers correctly.

Gap 4 occurs, for example, where external communications are an important part of the service provided. Companies may not inform customers of how hard they are trying to guarantee the quality of the service.

Parasuraman et al.'s (1985) conceptual framework (Figure 4.1) summarises the determinants of service quality and this framework is often referred to as the 'SERVQUAL' scale. Furthermore, their study identified ten 'determinants of perceived service quality' which they suggested consumers used to form their expectations and perceptions of the services they receive. These determinants were:

access	which involves how approachable the service provider is and how easy it is to contact them
communication	keeping customers informed in a language that they can understand (Ford used this determinant in her research)
competence	or the possession of the skills and knowledge required to perform the service
courtesy	the politeness, respect, consideration and friendliness of service personnel
credibility	how trustworthy, believable and honest employees seem to be
reliability	the consistency and dependability of service performance
responsiveness	how ready and willing employees are to provide the service the consumer requires
security	whether the consumer feels that purchasing the service leaves them free from danger, risk or doubt
tangibles	the physical aspects of the service
understanding/knowing the customer	how the service provider makes an effort to understand their customers' needs.

Moments of truth

Service expectations inform customer perceptions and the experience of the actual service encounter informs and enables consumers to learn about providers' abilities to meet their individual expectations. Moments of truth are critical points in the customer's experience when critical impressions are formed that will inform a consumer's further behaviour.

Jan Carlzon took over running Scandinavian Airlines (SAS) late in the 1970s and at the time the airline was failing financially and in terms of customer service as flights were regularly late. Carlzon's understanding of the hospitality industry and the importance of customer service helped him transform the airline industry. Among the many changes he made, he noticed critical moments of time when customers form good or bad impressions about a brand or service provider, for example, first impressions and handling of complaints.

Carlzon is widely quoted as saying:

> Last year, each of our ten million customers came in contact with approximately five SAS employees, and this contact lasted an average of 15 seconds each time. The SAS decisive moment is 'created' 50 million times a year, 15 seconds at a time. These 50 million 'moments of truth' are the moments that ultimately determine whether SAS will succeed or fail as a company. They are the moments when we must prove to our customers that SAS is their best alternative.

> (Carlzon, 1987, p. 3)

The implications for retail managers are that they should analyse customer interactions throughout the operation and identify potential break points and 'moment of truth' opportunities.

What happens when service encounters go wrong?

Another important stream of research examines what happens when customers are dissatisfied with the service that they receive. One outcome is that these customers may choose to take their business elsewhere.

In 1984, Fornell and Wernerfelt (1987) explored the management of customer complaints and found complaints could be used as part of a 'defensive' marketing strategy: to retain dissatisfied customers.

They suggested that organisations which paid careful attention to their customers' complaints could use analysis of complaints to prevent both current and new competitors from taking customers away. These marketing academics argued that, contrary to popular belief, businesses ought to try to increase the number of customer complaints they receive. At first glance, this idea may strike you as somewhat ridiculous. So it is worthwhile spending some time considering exactly what they meant by this and to understand why it might not be such a bad idea after all.

Fornell and Wernerfelt's central argument is that by retaining dissatisfied customers, firms can improve their market share, improve their profits and lower the costs of offensive marketing (trying to win new customers). Offensive marketing such as promotional campaigns in larger retailers is often determined by staff in a centralised function and may require little direct in-store involvement. The battle to retain satisfied customers and attract dissatisfied customers, however, is won in-store.

It is no surprise that customers who are dissatisfied with the service they receive sometimes complain. According to Singh (1988), their complaints may be divided into three different types:

- Customers may complain to the retailer or to the manufacturer formally. This is referred to as a 'voice response'.

- Customers may complain in an informal manner to people that are not directly involved in the interaction, for example their friends and relatives. This is a 'private response'.

- Customers may complain to a third party, such as a newspaper or a legal representative. Complaint behaviour such as this is described as a 'third-party response'.

With the rise of social networking sites it's possible that these two last forms of complaint have become even more influential in recent years. These three complaint options are shown in Figure 4.2.

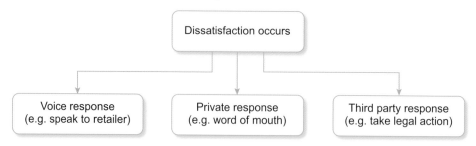

Figure 4.2 Some types of customer complaints

In summary, Fornell and Wernerfelt (1987) argued that business is lost if customers are encouraged not to voice their concerns. Although their analysis was less detailed than that of Singh (1988), they maintained that it is in the interests of the company to encourage customers to complain directly when they are dissatisfied and that, through careful, cost-effective analysis, the retailer may then act to sort things out.

Activity 4.3 Complaints

Spend about 20 minutes on this activity.

Purpose: to reflect on the ways in which you complain.

Task: Think about an occasion when you were dissatisfied with the service that you received from a retailer and make brief notes in answer to the following questions:

1 Who did you complain to and why?

2 What would have encouraged you to complain in a different way?

Feedback

I recently switched my broadband internet account from one service provider to another. Whilst the new company sent me the equipment on the date agreed and the service was available as and when I expected, I was dissatisfied with the automated telephone call I received which informed me that my new account was 'live'. At this point I would have liked to speak to a 'real' person about some other technical problems that I was experiencing with the mobile broadband service.

In this instance, I didn't complain to anyone at the company concerned, although my husband was well aware of the problem that I was having. This is an example of a private complaint. If I had been able to voice my concerns to the company, it might have been able to improve its service by changing the instructions it sent out with the mobile equipment. As it is, the company remained unaware that I was unhappy with their service.

Had I been able to speak to a person, rather than simply given an automated voice message, it is quite likely that I would have asked for some help – and indeed I may even have received some – which would have enhanced my view of the quality of service offered.

Although you will have described a different incident as part of the Activity 4.3, you may find that some of the points you thought of were similar to those in my feedback.

So far in this session we have examined a number of important factors relating to customer service from the retailers' perspective. You have seen some of the difficulties associated with generating robust shopper typologies and looked at how retailers might identify the service expectations that different types of customers may have so that they can target their service delivery most effectively. These theories may be useful for identifying those features which are of particular importance in a range of customer service contexts. The final area we consider is organisational culture and possible impacts on business performance.

4.3 Employee culture change at Sears

The mini-case below draws on studies conducted by Rucci et al. (1998). It describes how Sears Roebuck, a large US retailer, placed renewed emphasis on employee communications to improve what had been a lacklustre business performance. These changes were attributed primarily to its strategy of reorganising the business around the customer. This case explores how employee culture was changed at Sears.

Human resource management at Sears

Sears, Roebuck & Company was incorporated in 1886 and is a US retailing giant. Following a lapse into unprofitability in the early 1990s, in 1996 the firm undertook a major reorganisation which left it with five distinct business units. These included 'full-line' stores (which employed approximately 250,000 employees); home or 'off the mall' stores; an automotive division of 35,000 employees; speciality stores, which employed approximately 10,000 employees and a Sears credit services division of around 12,000 people.

Arthur Martinez, the Chief Executive Officer (CEO) at the time stated, 'a hallmark of great companies is an ability to recognise the game has changed and to adapt'. As part of Sears' adaptation, Sears' employees were re-educated to engage successfully in a business in which risk-taking and market-orientated innovation were encouraged. This was a dramatic departure from its previous 'command and control' management approach. This company-wide re-orientation was driven by a rhetoric which placed the customer – identified as a wealthy, middle-class American 'mom' – at the heart of the business.

In part, this change was achieved through a new, clarified vision announced to all employees, more resources targeted in stores and a decentralised approach to human resource management. Employees were encouraged to engage actively with these changes in the business and to take out a personal, financial stake in its success.

Reflecting upon their accomplishments in altering the culture of the company, senior managers identified five key changes, which, they believed had helped them to turn the company around financially.

The first of these changes involved the formulation and communication of a corporate mission, vision and goals.

Corporate mission, vision and goals

Rather than a conventional mission and value statement, Sears developed a conceptual model (see Figure 4.3) which linked employees, customers and shareholders. This model captured Sears' three aims of:

- creating a compelling place to work
- creating a compelling place to shop
- creating a compelling place to invest.

Figure 4.3 Sears' initial employee–customer–profit model: from objectives to measures

Information related to two trading quarters was compiled across 800 different stores. Surveys of employees and customers were combined with financial measures of performance. This data was used to develop the initial model shown in the figure through the use of a sophisticated computer modelling method called econometric causal pathway analysis. The results suggested that there were links between employee satisfaction, customer satisfaction and business performance.

Employee education and development

The second change came in the form of employee education and development. Sears' financial results were presented to the workforce on a quarterly and on an annual basis. Based upon recent local figures, employees were also set 'target' and 'stretch' goals.

Though initially unanticipated, managers felt that the focus groups they created to communicate this information to employees were the second element of importance. These group meetings revealed how few Sears' employees understood the financial and operations aspects of business.

Human resource specialists developed a series of 'learning maps' to change this situation. These large, colourful, graphic posters illustrated topics such as:

- 'Ownership', how does it create value and what effect does it have on shareholder wealth?

- 'Total performance indicators', including the interrelationships between the three aspects of the model.

- 'A new day on retail street', which illustrated changes in the retailing industry.

- 'Voices of our customers', describing changing customer demographics and product/service choice processes of Sears' customers.

- 'The Sears money flow', detailing how each dollar of revenue was spent.

A third element of the cultural change experienced was the introduction of performance management and incentive compensation systems which human resource specialists linked closely to Sears' new strategy.

The fourth element identified was a set of 'validated' employee selection systems. These included the use of standardised, structured interview guides for a variety of positions. Selection tools were devised to assess applicants' 'customer service aptitude'.

The fifth element was described as delivering the 'HR basics' very competently. This involved the efficient and effective delivery of basic transactional systems. [Unfortunately, the study is unclear about precisely which systems the Sears management team considered these were.]

(Source: Extracted from Kirn, et al. (1999))

Case debrief

The case shows how Sears employees were encouraged to take risks and to develop a service offering which focused on its target market customer: typically a wealthy, middle-class female American shopper. Additionally, managers identified five key changes that were important for turning the business around:

1 The formulation and communication of a corporate mission, vision and goals. These were captured in the model as 'a compelling place to work', 'a compelling place to shop' and 'a compelling place to invest'.

2 Employee education and development through focus groups.

3 The introduction of performance management and incentive compensation systems.

4 Deployment of a set of validated selection systems.

5 Competent delivery of the 'HR basics' (although there is little information provided about what these were).

The Sears 'employee–customer–profit chain' is a retail-specific model generated from practices at one particular retailer – albeit across a very large number of stores indeed. As such, it may be appropriate for similar retail settings. You may, for instance, recognise a parallel between the Sears approach and those of the retailers featured in the multimedia activities which you did in Session 1 of this block. However, research in the service operations management field suggests that, even in very similar service settings, there is no guarantee that a focus on employee involvement and customer service produces superior business performance.

4.4 Conclusions

In this study session we have explored the concept of customer service and in doing so we have looked at types of consumers and their shopping missions. Second, we have identified types of retail customer service offerings and considered levels of customer service. Finally, we explored the concept of service encounters and looked in more detail at underlying research which aids our understanding of the breadth and scope of the service encounter. This session has identified many important management issues in the area of customer service management. We hope that you can see already that, whilst retailers may be interested in tailoring the customer service they provide to these different needs and desires, this may be more difficult than the theory suggests.

Learning outcomes

When you have completed all the study elements for this session, you should be able to:

- explain the difference between shopper types and shopping missions
- demonstrate your understanding of the concept of customer service
- discuss the importance of the customer service concept in retail management contexts.
- explain how customer service works in a variety of retail contexts
- reflect on your own experience when carrying out activities
- consider the relevance of employee satisfaction to customer satisfaction and business performance.

Session 5 Managing a retail store

In this final session we will examine some important retail processes, including some of the practicalities related to inventory and visual merchandise management. We will also look at how the availability of detailed electronic point-of-sale (EPOS) information has contributed to customer relationship management – a topic which will be developed further in Block 3. The adoption of information systems is not without problems, and we will discuss some of these, notably the problem of 'retail shrinkage' measurement.

5.1 Day-to-day operations

Retailing is an ever-changing business with tasks and priorities often changing daily. Responsibility for the day-to-day operations of a store lies with the store manager. We looked at some general management skills and HRM activities in the previous sessions of this book but we can see from the table below that a store manager's duties extend well beyond the management of staff.

Duties of the store manager

A manager working for a multiple retailer must put into full and effective operation in the branch at all times the company's policies and procedures. The day-to-day operations of the branch must be organised and directed to its full trading potential within the constraints of position and size of unit.

Table 5.1 A store manager's duties

Sales	Achieve budgeted sales.
Costs	Maintain controllable costs within a budget (e.g., lighting, telephones).
Profit	Achieve planned levels of profit, both gross and net, for the period.
Stock	Maintain a level of stock within the current budget; to keep stock shortages to a minimum; to count and record stock in the branch from time to time as required by company policy.
Buying	Ensure that if local buying is permitted, purchases are made only in line with company policy, taking into account the total budgeted stock holding.
Presentation	Maintain standards of display and presentation that encourage retail trade and contribute to the identity the company wishes to project. This entails: sales areas, windows, shop fronts to be maintained in a clean and tidy condition (this also applies to stock areas, staffrooms and toilets); all merchandise is displayed in line with company standards including the open display lines appropriate to all grades of branch, the correct price marking and ticketing of products.

Sales promotions	Carry out the company sales promotions policy and to initiate and execute local sales promotions in agreement with the area manager.
Staff	Ensure by interview and selection (agreed with the area manager) that the branch is properly staffed to its budgeted establishment with competent section management and assistance; to train staff in the basic functions of branch operations; to terminate their employment within the scope of the company policy and with regard to legislation.
Premises	Protect and maintain the building machinery equipment, fixtures, fitting and vehicles at the branch and to report any action needed to maintain trade assets in good working order and at acceptable safety standards.
Administration	Carry out procedures as published from time to time for the reception and disposition of safe custody of cash stock and other assets; to prepare, maintain and submit such records and reports as may from time to time be required by the company; to observe the large amount of legislation that surrounds retailing.
Communication	Establish and maintain adequate means of communication within the branch of the company's objectives as they affect branch personnel, including in-store meetings; to keep area mangers aware as far as possible of local news and developments likely to affect the company's present and future interests; to play an active part, as far as it is feasible, in the civic and cultural activities of the locality in which the branch is sited in order to foster confidence and goodwill towards the company.

(Source: Cox and Brittain, 2003, p. 260–2.)

Please note that this extensive list of tasks is equally applicable to the independent store owner/manager.

From the unit (branch) manager's perspective many of these tasks relate to budgetary and quantifiable activities. Efficient managers need to be able to implement and manage performance standards across a range of activities.

Measuring a manager's performance

A store manager's performance is measured on trading and management skills. Trading skills refer to the ability to spot opportunities within the retail business environment in order to maximise store profits. Management skills are concerned with maximising the resource under the manager's control. The manager has to work out how to balance the demands of the customers against the capacity of the store, which in terms of performance measurement means managing store assets to achieve the best possible performance at an optimum cost under the headings of:

customers

merchandise

store workforce

store physical resource (including actual retail space).

Measuring store productivity

The most effective way of measuring productivity is to calculate ratios of resource to results, such as profit per square metre of selling space. Then compare these ratios with budgets and other performance plans. Some of the ratios used to measure performance are so well established that it is possible to compare, say, productivity levels against industry norms. In other words, how is a particular store performing against similar stores across the retail industry?

Important measures of store productivity are shown in Table 5.2

Table 5.2 Measures of productivity

Area of the business	Performance measure
Sales	Sales per hour
	Sales per employee
Staff	Labour cost per activity
	Staff cost as a percentage of sales
	Average wage cost per hour
Customers	Sales per customer (by value, number of items or department)
Merchandise	Items per time period
Space	Sales per metre of selling space
	Sales per checkout
	Sales per linear meter of fixture
General management	Gross margin return on investments
	Gross profit margin per square metre
	Net profit per square metre
	Shrinkage as a percentage of sales
	Wastage as a percentage of sales
	Mark-downs as a percentage of sales

There are other qualitative measures such as service to customers and merchandise availability but these are less straightforward to measure, but the level of customer complaints may be an indicator. Stock–age rating is also important to identify slow moving stock, which unnecessarily ties up capital or requires mark down, thus reducing profitability.

As an example, a typical grocery multiple will have a gross profit on sales of approximately 17 per cent. Staff costs will typically run at 5–6 per cent and other operating costs 2–3 per cent. With overhead and allocated costs of 4–5 per cent it can be demonstrated that net profits are in the order of 4–5 per cent of sales. Therefore, it is clear that saving in staff and operation costs (controllable by the operating manager) can have a dramatic effect on a branch's profitability and the profit of the business as a whole.

5.2 Visual merchandising, space productivity and replenishment

This section is concerned with merchandising practices in department store concessions, measures taken by some grocery retailers to improve space productivity and the difficulties of efficient replenishment in some product areas of the UK do-it-yourself (DIY) sector. We start with a brief look at some of the principles of in-store merchandising.

Merchandise display refers to the way in which products presented for sale are displayed in-store.

Visual merchandising has been defined as 'activity which coordinates effective merchandise selection with effective merchandise display' (Walters and White, 1987, p. 238 cited in Kerfoot et al., 2003). Researchers have considered various aspects of the visual merchandising management function, notably: layout, fixtures, product selection, techniques for merchandise planning and presentation, and in-store packaging requirements.

One useful way of thinking about the different aspects that make up in-store visual displays is the classification scheme offered by Omar (1999, cited in Kerfoot et al., 2003). This scheme divides the elements of visual merchandising into three areas:

- architectural, building-based elements
- point-of-sale displays (at till-points for example)
- merchandise display.

A particularly important area here relates to the amount of space allocated to a given product. You will read more about this aspect of retail planning in Book 4.

Visual merchandising may seem to be more important in some retail sectors than others. For example, fashion and home-furnishing retailers have always devoted considerable resources to displaying products in a visually appealing way, whilst discount grocery retailers may be more concerned about space, productivity and efficiency. Likewise, responsibility for visual merchandising varies from being part of the remit of corporate communications, promotion or marketing to being a separate role at board level (Lea-Greenwood, 1998).

One of the perceived advantages of using centralised teams is that the retail brand identity can be controlled across all outlets, and visual merchandising can tie in with other corporate communication themes and messages. There is, however, a danger that the centralised approach may prevent the retailer from adapting visual-merchandising activities to reflect local themes, preferences and competition. Sometimes a multi-outlet retailer may use a team of regional merchandisers who travel between the retailers' stores within a given area.

We will look next at an example of the approach to visual merchandising taken in women's fashion retail.

Merchandising for brand impact in women's fashion retail concessions

Concession retailing in a department store is interesting because concessionary brand retailers have to present their merchandise distinctively within a cluttered retail environment of a store, which also accommodates the department store's own-branded merchandise and own-bought merchandise.

Branded fashion concession (Autumn 2006) in a UK department store

The work by Kerfoot et al. (2003) mentioned above examined the link between visual merchandising methods and customers' purchasing behaviour. Although a customer's reaction to the display did not determine whether she made a purchase, the findings suggest that customers who liked it were four times more likely to make a purchase than those who did not.

The aspects of visual merchandising that seemed to have the most influence on the consumers' purchasing intentions were: colour, presentation style, awareness of fixtures (e.g., the creation of a high-quality image through the use of wooden hangers), path finding, and the sensory qualities of the materials and the lighting.

Kerfoot et al. suggested the use of 'facet' theory for the design of customer questionnaires. This is a structured method for clarifying the best questions to ask in order to establish which aspects (or facets) of visual display are the most important to customers' perceptions about a brand. You may like to try out this approach for yourself. Now let's move on to another example, again from the UK grocery sector.

Activity 5.1 Merchandising fast-moving goods in the grocery sector

Spend about 30 minutes on this activity

Purpose: to consider the implications of product packaging and design of fast-moving consumer goods (FMCG).

Task: Read Box 5.1 'Shelf-ready packaging'. In this article, which was written in 2005, Elaine Watson suggests that some manufacturers may be put under severe financial pressure to meet Tesco's demands for shelf-ready packaging (SRP).

As you read:

1   Identify the various people who were asked to comment and the stakeholder groups they represent.

2   Make a brief note of how their views on the shelf-ready packaging initiative introduced by Tesco differ.

Shelf-ready packaging is a term used to describe the preparation and presentation of products in such a way that operations carried out previously by retailers are transferred to their manufacturing suppliers. This is another example of the blurring of the boundary between products and services that you read about in Book 1.

Box 5.1 Shelf-ready packaging

Manufacturers commented as Tesco unveiled plans to push 10,000 chilled, ambient and fresh products into SRP by the end of the year in a radical bid to boost availability.

Sainsbury, Asda, Somerfield and other large UK grocer retailers, called also for more products to go into merchandising units and demanded smaller case sizes to ease their in-store replenishment processes.

One supplier, who asked not to be named, said: 'If you're talking about merchandising units, this will push significant costs upstream. It may be that you have to introduce another link to the supply chain managed by a third party to supply goods in this way.'

However, Tesco's category director for bakery, Tony Reed, said that the business case would become apparent to suppliers in the longer term, but insisted SRP was a 'no brainer'. He added: 'If you can identify products in the backroom, get them on to the shop floor quickly and get them straight on to shelf, everyone benefits.'

The Milk Link group supply chain director, David Coleman, said: 'There is a perception that the supplier pays and that the retailer reaps the rewards, but we both benefit from better availability. For Tesco SRP is a priority, whilst Asda has been more focused on case sizes.'

The Müller Dairy UK supply chain development manager, Keith Hallam, added: 'It's been largely positive for us, but SRP raises lots of issues, for example, space planning systems need to account for the room taken up by a shelf-ready tray, or products don't fit on to shelves anymore.'

A new shelf-ready toolkit available at tescodesign.com has been created to help suppliers get to grips with Tesco's requirements when reformulating products or approaching a range review, said Tony Reed. He added,

'Frozen is a tough category to crack. Cardboard must be able to cope with freezer temperatures and the automatic transport systems in distribution centres. We're working with a couple of own-label suppliers on this.'

A supermarket employee pushing shelf-ready packaging

Wheeled units that can be rolled straight on to the shop floor are only suitable for fast selling lines such as milk, wine on promotion, soft drinks, sugar and bananas, he said. 'Then you've got re-usable green trays and cardboard trays that slide straight onto the shelf.'

Biscuits would be in cardboard tray packs in a couple of months, while bread remained 'work in progress'. He said. 'In the 53 stores where we have been trialling plastic trays for bread, suppliers have seen real benefits from increased sales.'

(Source: Watson, 2005)

Feedback

The article discusses the shelf-ready packaging initiative from a number of different viewpoints. Senior representatives from retailers and suppliers express their opinions. No store employee opinions are quoted, yet arguably it is these people whose working lives are the most affected. Interestingly, the supplier who expressed a negative view seems to have asked not to be named. Other supplier representatives, from the body representing dairy supply businesses, were generally positive about the changes. It may be that some of the reasons for this diversity of opinion are due to technical challenges related to particular types of products – and discussed in detail by one of Tesco's category directors, Tony Reed. An alternative, and perhaps more convincing, explanation centres on the significant purchasing power of United Kingdom grocery retailers.

We will explore how retailers and their suppliers manage supply management in more detail in Book 4.

5.3 Stock management: The management of replenishment by supplier-employed specialists

A study examined the in-store merchandising practices of two large-format DIY retailers (Emberson et al., 2006). Two merchandising teams employed by the suppliers were used to supplement in-store merchandising activities for a subset of the retailers' timber product range.

These raw, machined and moulded timber products were particularly difficult to merchandise, not least because of their awkward bulk. They came in a multitude of sizes, which customers would often mix up and, as timber is a live material, the timber from which they were made was prone to warp, bend or get damaged whilst on in-store display. Sorting the timber of merchantable quality from that which needed to be discarded required an experienced eye. The use of supplier-employed merchandisers extended the manufacturer's remit from that of a product supplier to that of a provider of product services.

Members of these merchandising teams were dedicated to the stores of a certain retail chain within a prescribed geographical area. They were responsible for a range of in-store tasks, including replenishment, quality control and management reporting. Whilst they represented the supplier in a sales capacity, they worked alongside in-store employees carrying out timber quality audits, product availability checks and merchandising the timber display if required.

Interestingly, the study found that there were significant differences between merchandisers' and retail store managers' perceptions of these merchandisers' roles and their respective merchandising competencies. Supplier-employed merchandisers were more confident about their timber-merchandising experience than in-store employees. This is hardly surprising, given that the supplier merchandisers were well-trained timber specialists, many of whom had over two years' experience in their roles.

Despite these higher competency levels, however, and notwithstanding the formal approval of their presence in-store by the DIY store's head office buyers, in-store personnel were dismissive. Store employees were sensitive to merchandisers' advice which they often perceived as critical of their own, in-store merchandising practices. Out-of-stock observations were deflected as 'supplier problems' and, if the shelves were empty when supplier merchandisers visited and on close inspection found stock available elsewhere, this news was not well received. As one store duty manager commented, 'There's always a reason why it's not put away, either we're too busy or whatever' (Emberson et al., 2006, p. 478). Indeed some store managers went as far as to nickname observation reports from the supplier merchandisers as the 'shaft' reports.

DIY retail store managers were responsible for a stock portfolio that ran into thousands of units (these are individual product lines, often referred to as 'stock-keeping units' or SKUs). Timber product merchandising was not unduly high on their priority list. Yet this type of sporadic attention to stock availability has unintended consequences.

The implementation of information-based sales and stock-planning systems has been as ubiquitous in DIY retail as elsewhere. These systems promise sales performance improvements through better on-shelf availability. Sophisticated computer algorithms are used to calculate the replenishment stock required. However, the data on which this replenishment is based – and which is used to calculate the sales forecasts and purchase orders – is prone to inaccuracies if store stocks are merchandised ineffectively. Indeed, things may only get worse. As one supplier merchandiser commented, 'All the technologies in the world won't help you if you don't have the business disciplines' (Emberson et al., 2006, p. 478).

In the next section we will examine another practical issue of relevance to the accuracy of information system data: retail shrinkage.

5.4 A framework for the assessment of retail shrinkage

'Shrinkage' is the term given to the reduction in inventory through factors such as shoplifting, employee theft, paperwork errors and supplier fraud. This section will look at this concept and explore some methods that have been employed in order to counter shrinkage.

Activity 5.2 Retail Shrinkage

Spend about 30 minutes on this activity.

Purpose: to introduce the concept of retail 'shrinkage'.

Task: Read Box 5.2 entitled 'Razor blade shrinkage' and make notes on why you think the retailer chose to display its razor blade products in this way.

Box 5.2 Razor blade shrinkage

A study conducted in 2007 across several, large US grocery retail stores claims to have found that high-theft security devices provide a drop in shrinkage and a rise in the sales of razor blades.

The study was conducted by exploring the application, interpretation and presentation of numerical data in a way appropriate to context, said an expert in retail security and loss prevention.

It assessed the effectiveness of a 'keeper' system (large plastic boxes in which products can be seen clearly) in reducing shrinkage, increasing sales and in preventing out-of-stock occurrences. The perceptions of retail customers and employees were also canvassed.

Keepers, clear polycarbonate cases with specialised electronics, are designed specifically to protect high-theft merchandise. The merchandise is kept safe whilst allowing customers to browse the shelves and visually examine the products inside. This enables customers to make purchasing decisions much more easily than would be the case if these products were located in another area of the store, inside a locked cabinet, behind a sales desk, or if the customer required the assistance of a store employee to examine the product – adding time and hassle to the customers' shopping experience. Instead, even in a keeper case, customers can take the products off the shelves to examine them and carry them to the cash register, where the check-out employee may unlock the case.

The results of this study, which involved the use of Keepers to merchandise nearly 70 different wet shaving blade and razor products, showed that this method of protection significantly reduced shrinkage and also increased sales compared with the normal options of control used by these stores. In each of the test stores, shrink was significantly lower, and positive effects increased as time elapsed.

For instance, product sales increased due to better on-shelf availability. In-store associates had to assist fewer customers and there was a decrease in the recorded incidents of out-of-stock merchandise. When factors such as the costs of goods, reduced shrink, increased sales, cost of labour, cost of capital, time and out-of-stocks are measured, the study suggested that Keepers could pay for themselves in around seven months.

The study reported also that retail customers found it easy to select and access the appropriate merchandise, and that they reacted positively to the aesthetic Keeper design. On-shelf access was appreciated and a number of customers reported the benefits of not needing to seek assistance from store employees to get the product from another area of the store or to unlock a cabinet.

Check-out cashiers noticed more razors coming through the check-out lines due to the improved on-shelf availability. They stated that Keepers were easy to use and required minimal additional time to unlock and remove products. So, those employees and customers interviewed seemed to affirm that: 'Keeper systems are an excellent combination of security and accessibility'.

Source: adapted from SecurityPark.net, 2008.

Feedback

Razor blades are a very small, high-value product which conventional wisdom suggests may be easily stolen. It is interesting, therefore, that this is the product chosen by these retailers to trial. Whilst no mention is made of the reasons for research into this product category, retail managers may do well to consider carefully how they can best target interventions to reduce retail shrinkage levels.

According to Chapman and Templar (2006, pp. 860–72), the first academic reports of retail shrinkage date back to the 1960s. Yet these authors stated that shrinkage in the grocery sector alone was still estimated to cost European retailers €24 billion in 2003.

As indicated in Box 5.2, shrinkage is something of a double whammy in that it may both increase retail costs and threaten sales. But how can shrinkage be defined? You can read what Chapman and Templar have to say about this in the extract in Box 5.3 entitled 'Delimiting shrinkage'.

Box 5.3 Delimiting shrinkage

Clarity and consistency are required when measuring [shrinkage] in order to ensure that like is measured with like and that each measurement is compatible. Hence there is a need to delimit the term 'shrinkage' and to do so in a simple and clear manner.

In a simplistic view, the value of a product is a function of several factors including its being in the right place at the right time and possessing an appropriate level of quality. [You will read more about these marketing aspects in Book 3.] This value will be compromised if these factors fail to meet customer expectations. For example, if a product is damaged and its quality is compromised so its value will be reduced. Similarly, value can be reduced if goods are not available at the right time or if they are not in the right place.

In the grocery retail environment the value of a good is represented by its intended sale price. Any loss of value in a product is assumed here to be represented through a mark down in its sale price.

The most extreme reduction in [product] value is when it is reduced to zero by writing off the product when it can no longer be sold. This can happen for the reasons described above and also when goods cannot be physically accounted for. Goods that cannot be accounted for will be identified where there is a discrepancy between book stock and physical stock. The book stock is the record of those goods held by the company and calculated as follows:

Book stock = Results from the last physical stock count + net movements

where,

> Net movements = (purchases + incoming transfers) − (sales +
> outgoing transfers)

Discrepancies between book stock and physical stock will come to light following a physical audit of a company's goods, such as a stock take. In a stock take the goods physically recorded in the audit are compared to the book stock and differences are recorded.

A retailer incurs a loss when a good is sold for less than its intended price, i.e. there is some intended sales income that was not realised and also when the intended sales income from products cannot be realised because of stock loss. It is proposed that these losses are what lie at the heart of the shrinkage issue. Therefore shrinkage will be delimited here as relating to:

> Intended sales income that was not and cannot be realised.

This definition is intended to be clear and simple. This should allow the concept of shrinkage to be more easily communicated to the broad range of people that need to be engaged in addressing it.

> (Source: Chapman and Templar, 2006, pp. 860–72)

Shrinkage problems have been linked to particular products (e.g., razor blades, alcohol), locations, processes (e.g., goods receipt, self-checkout), types of people (e.g., internal employees, shoplifters, suppliers) and times (e.g., store closure, early morning when the store is quieter, or lunchtime, when the store may be at its busiest). Despite the frightening size of some retail shrinkage estimates, gathering data about shrinkage is itself a costly exercise. For these reasons, Chapman and Templar attempted to be clear and concise in their definition. They went on to propose three major areas on which retailers might concentrate their data measurement and comparison in order to reduce shrinkage: stewardship and performance improvement, cost reduction and sales improvement, and the local effects of systemic issues.

Stewardship and performance improvement

Stewardship is the safe and conservative running of in-store operations along prescribed lines.

Chapman and Templar suggested that, first, a retail store needs to make a conservative estimate of the value of the goods it sells. This may be the lower of either the purchase cost or the net realisable value. Use of the goods' selling price would inflate this aspect of shrinkage and skew later comparisons.

Net realisable value is the amount which assets can be sold for, minus the costs involved in selling the assets.

Performance improvement implies a change to maximise business returns. In terms of shrinkage, therefore, it means that the retail store needs to highlight the profit lost as a result of any shrinkage and not, as many retailers may do, focus on the sales value of the products that have disappeared.

Cost reduction and sales improvement

Reducing the cost of shrinkage may enable profit to be increased. The costs of dealing with shrinkage include the cost of measuring shrinkage itself, and the costs of installing and maintaining security equipment, paying store detectives and security guards, and providing security-tagged products.

Some of the benefits of reducing shrinkage that were identified by Chapman and Templar are presented in Table 5.3.

Table 5.3 Opportunities for reducing shrinkage and improving sales

Characteristic	Sales improvement opportunities from shrinkage reduction
Value for money shopping	Reduction in shrinkage costs and cost-effective shrinkage management leveraged to reduce price of goods and drive sales.
On-shelf availability	Automated store replenishment triggers reordering when sales reduce recorded inventory below a threshold. Shrinkage can cause stock-outs to occur before the inventory reordering threshold is reached. Once this situation is reached further sales cannot occur. Replenishment will not be triggered until the inventory record is manually reset.
One-stop shopping	Fear of shrinkage can prevent retailers stocking items perceived as being at risk. Overcoming the threat of shrinkage encourages the retailer to stock a wide assortment.
Good shopping experience	Fear of shrinkage can lead retailers to defensively merchandise products. Removing the causes of shrinkage and implementing alternative solutions that counter the threat of shrinkage can allow goods to be openly merchandised. Open merchandising improves the shopping experience and tends to increase sales.
Safe visit	Overt security measures and a hard-line attitude by employees can promote a perception amongst shoppers that there is a threat to safety. Sensitive yet robust operations management can provide a safe environment in which to work and shop that is compatible with a good shopping experience.

(Source: Chapman and Templar, 2006, pp. 860–72)

The local effects of systemic issues

According to Chapman and Templar, a systemic approach to shrinkage management leads to a view of shrinkage as the symptom of a range of issues. They illustrated this point with the following example:

> Take, for example, the response when a case of bottles is dropped in the back of [the] store. Taken in isolation, a localised view of shrinkage may result in the employee who dropped the case being reprimanded and the broken items cleared away. Viewed from a systemic perspective, this same incident is seen as being the consequence of several factors that combined in a critical way at the time of the

incident. For example, the case of bottles was half full and unstable; the employee was in a hurry as they had been called away from shelf replenishment to serve on the busy checkouts; when the case of bottles was dropped, the employee was holding the case in one hand while using the other hand to make space on an already full warehouse shelf. None of these factors were individually critical but they conspired in a way that led to the incident.

(Chapman and Templar, 2006, p. 867)

The authors believe that the management ability to evaluate this incident in these broader terms might mean that subsequent shrinkage losses could be reduced. They suggest that this broader view might require attention to corporate policies on product design, replenishment quantity and frequency, facility layouts and recruitment, as well as staff discipline.

Technology has a huge role to play in monitoring shrinkage. As we will see in the next session, the implications of technology can also be felt when looking at a retailer's relationship with its customers.

5.5 Technology in retail stores: data and customer relationship management

In this section, we focus on how retailers use in-store information systems and reflect on how electronic data capture of individual customers' purchasing transactions has developed into a sophisticated set of tools for customer relationship management (CRM). This builds on your studies of barcodes and associated technology in Multimedia activities 2 and incorporates the ethics and sustainability theme case for Block 2.

Customer relationship management (CRM)

New and innovative technologies are helping retailers develop sophisticated customer relationship management (CRM) systems. Researchers (Zablah et al. 2004, p. 475), suggest CRM is defined as the management of a mutually beneficial relationship between customer and supplier and may be viewed as a continuous process, which enables retailers to use data to select and develop long-term relationships with their most profitable customers.

However, to achieve the potential benefits of adopting a CRM system requires more than setting up the technology to gather and analyse customer data. Zablah et al. (2004), argue that a retailer needs to invest in a number of resources (capital equipment, employee skills, intellectual property, etc.) in order to meet the changing needs of their customers, which form the basis of a good CRM system. If a retailer has the right resources and capabilities, they should be able to continually modify how they respond towards individual customers by anticipating how customers' needs may change. Therefore an effective CRM system needs to gather intelligence about current and prospective customers, apply this intelligence to reshape the organisation's and its employees' behaviours towards these customers and apply appropriate technology. This enables retailers and supplier analysts to 'build knowledge' at various stages along the supply chain from manufacture to consumption, in order to maximise sales through development of close connective relationships with the customer.

Additionally, CRM can be considered as an underlying philosophy, which enables a company (retailer) to establish and develop strategies to encourage customer loyalty and long-term relationships (Zablah et al., 2004). The lifetime customer value, which Smith (2010) defines as the value of a customer to the retailer based on how much money they will spend in the store over all their visits during their lifetime against the cost of keeping that customer, is an important indicator of the value of customer relationships. Customer lifetime value is also an important part of CRM as it infers that a buyer–seller relationship is more than a one-off transaction between a buyer and a seller; in other words, there is a sense of an ongoing relationship, which can be nurtured and maintained, whilst it is agreeable and beneficial for both parties.

A good example of the application of the CRM philosophy is the continuing interest shown, by grocery retailers especially, in card-based customer loyalty programmes).

Box 5.4 Promotional offers related to the Tesco Clubcard

During the process of developing their EPOS data warehouse, Tesco faced price competition from other leading grocery retailers. The traditional response to such moves by a competitor might be to lower prices across the board. However, this might mean that in order to retain price-sensitive customers (those who may be likely to defect to another store on the grounds of price alone) the company would be giving discounts on products bought by customers who were not likely to defect. In other words, which products to select for price reduction was important if Tesco were not simply to waste money by giving ineffective incentives.

By using its Clubcard data, Tesco segmented its customer base on the basis of shopping patterns over a period of time. From this it was able to establish those products which were bought largely by 'price-conscious' customers. If Tesco could offer discounts on these products, it would retain these customers without giving discounts to the customer who did not need incentives to remain loyal.

Tesco selected its own-brand value margarine, as it had identified from the data that this product was bought only by those customers likely to defect on grounds of price alone. A price cut on this product was relatively cheap but had the desired effect, of keeping the customers who were most likely to defect.

(Source: adapted from Mutch, 2008, p. 84)

Activity 5.3 CRM success factors

Spend about 10 minutes on this activity.

Purpose: to identify the factors a retailer needs to consider when implementing a CRM system.

Task: From your studies so far, suggest the most important considerations for a retailer when implementing a CRM system.

Feedback

In order to implement a successful CRM system there are many considerations, but perhaps the most important factors are to:

- have a customer focus, which then guides the development of the CRM system
- have a common database – an integrated information system that allows all the staff involved in dealing with the customer to have access to the customer information
- have an information system which is flexible, so that it can meet changing requirements both from operational and strategic perspectives.

 Sustainability and ethics ─────────────────────

By using databases, information systems and associated technology, large retailers are becoming adept at gathering, analysing and interpreting customer data and this helps them to devise effective CRM strategies. The ethics and sustainability theme for this block explores who benefits most from developing close relationships and considers relationship quality.

Activity 5.4 Relationship quality

Spend about 40 minutes on this activity.

Purpose: to consider what affects relationship quality in CRM systems.

Task: Read the case study and answer the questions below.

'The technology of loyalty cards allows retailers to transform cold data on consumer behaviour into warm relationships and eventually into a genuine customer loyalty founded on mutual understanding and trust.' (Mauri, 2003.) But who benefits the most? And is it ethical to use technological approaches to build relationships with consumers, when the main aim is to encourage them to buy more products?

Case study 5.1 'Developing relationships or spying on the customer for profit?'

In her study of customer loyalty transaction records, Rowley (2005) analysed her own supermarket, bank and telephone transactions to identify the data that each of these three organisations might hold about their customers. She found typically this would include:

- personal identifiers such as name, account number
- personal contact details such as address, telephone number and email address
- any personal data offered by the customer when completing registration forms (or other forms submitted for completion to the retailer).

and perhaps most significantly:

- transaction data relating to interactions with any organisation with which the customer has had financial dealings.

The transaction data is used by retailers to develop relationships with customers based on product associations. Rowley (2005) gives two examples of the way that a retail customer's transaction data can be used. The first relates to regular purchases of wine or nappies at her local supermarket:

Example 1

If I regularly purchase wine or nappies at my supermarket, then I am likely to be a candidate for either their wine club or their Toddler and Baby club. This means that I am suitable for participation in one of the supermarket's other loyalty initiatives, and provides the supermarket with the opportunity to engage me as a member of one of their customer communities, and to channel 'useful information' through my letterbox and computer screen. In short, encouraging people to purchase more is linked up with the concept of loyalty and relationships and is a complex process of engagement and persuasion. Data is the leverage to the commencement of such processes, which in turn may lead to enhanced knowledge.

Example 2

Rowley explains how her bank is part of a major retailing group. She outlines why there is a significant temptation for these independent company divisions to work together to capitalise on their competitive advantage. Between bank and the retail division, the organisation has a detailed profile of her income and outgoings. Even if only aggregated data were passed between them, such data could be used to profile her as a customer according to her income level or her employment category and to map her transaction data against these segments.

(Source: Rowley, 2005, p. 106)

Rowley's examples indicate the scope retailers have to utilise our personal data to develop loyalty schemes and CRM systems. There are many complex issues to consider if we are to reflect on the ethics of a loyalty scheme and who it benefits the most. There are financial rewards for both the buyer and the seller. A loyal customer returns regularly to the same store and rewards the retailer by making regular purchases, in return the retailer may provide tailored discounts to reward the regular customer. This is an example of behavioural loyalty, which according to Rowley (2005) is all that some organisations are interested in – but this is not the only type of relationship that retailers seek to develop as more complex relationships, based on attitudinal loyalty, can be encouraged. However, this approach requires understanding of the value creation process and the nature of the customer base.

Whichever type of data is at the heart of the CRM system, the quality of the relationship is likely to be fundamental to the overall success of retailers' CRM initiatives. According to Morgan and Hunt (1994), trust and commitment are important to developing relationships and trust only exists when one party has confidence in an exchange partner's reliability and integrity. Therefore, retailers' CRM initiatives rely on relational exchanges being characterised by high levels of trust that enables both parties to focus on longer-term benefits of the relationship. Research has also found commitment to be the key component of establishing and maintaining long-term relationships between business partners (Cater and Zabkar, 2008). Therefore, if retailers show differing levels of commitment at differing stages in the relationship this will affect the relationship quality and customer loyalty.

Activity 5.5 Trust and commitment

Spend about 30 minutes on this activity.

Purpose: to explore the notion of trust between retailer and consumer.

Task: Answer the questions below.

1   How can a retailer demonstrate trust to its customers?

2   What might you do if you lose your trust in a retailer?

3   Why might your commitment be important to a retailer?

Feedback

1 Retailers demonstrate trust in a number of ways, for example in terms of the use of data. Customers rely on retailers to: use their personal data in a controlled and safe manner and not to share the data with other institutions (unless agreed), offer consistent product quality, deal with any complaints effectively and provide products and services that are safe for consumption.

2 If you are prepared to trust a retailer, you are likely expect the company to reliably provide the products and services you require. Take your bank (a retail service provider), the majority of us trust banks to deal with our financial transactions with honesty and integrity. However, the economic collapse of 2008/9 revealed how some financial institutions had operated 'dubious' trading practices at high levels. This led to a questioning of financial integrity and lack of trust in major financial institutions which triggered a widespread collapse of financial systems. This is an extreme example but once a retailer loses your trust you are likely to shop elsewhere.

3 Retailers need regular customers as they rely on identifying purchasing patterns in order to provide appropriate goods and services at the right time and place. Without such commitment from customers to purchase items, retailers are unable plan effectively.

--- End of theme

 TGF activity

Now go to your tutor group forum and discuss the importance of trust and commitment between individual employees and a retail employer.

5.6 Conclusions

In this study session you have learnt about the duties of the store manager, visual merchandising, shrinkage, retail technology and considered the importance of relationship quality and how retailers use customer data to develop profitable relationships.

More specifically, you have seen that the mechanisation of retailing may extend all the way from the design of tasks conducted in-store, through to the prescription and monitoring of retail store managers' activities and performance. It is also increasingly being used to measure consumer behaviours.

Learning outcomes

When you have completed all the study elements for this session, you should be able to:

- describe the roles and responsibilities of retail store managers in various retail settings
- discuss the importance of merchandising
- understand and explain how to evaluate retail shrinkage rates so that retail managers actions may be effectively targeted
- understand and explain the importance of accurate data collection from information systems and its role in CRM processes.

You should have developed your learning by completing the activities and reflections in this study session.

This brings you to the end of Block 2. If you haven't already done so, turn now to the first tutor-marked assignment (TMA): You will find details of the TMA in your assignment resource on the B122 website.

Block 2 Conclusions

In this block, we have explored retail operations and looked at how store-based retail businesses work.

The main aims associated with your study of retail store operations were to:

- enable you to examine the diversity of management roles in retail stores
- explore the differences in management functions between the independent owner-managers of small business and retail franchises and managers of multi-outlet retail stores
- provide you with an overview of some important store management processes, including human resource management, the interactions between retailers and their customers
- observe the use and limitations of in-store retail information systems.

This block also provides an introduction to aspects of HRM which may be relevant to retail store managers.

Information system data forms the backbone of centralised retailers' customer relationship management systems. The use of EPOS data, for example, is central to retailers' success both in terms of sound financial control and future management decision making about the continuity and development of retail products and services. Furthermore, the application of technology to centralise and automate tasks such as inventory management, on-shelf planning and display has altered fundamentally the nature of in-store operations. These changes seem to have had far-reaching implications.

As you progress through the module you will learn also about retail planning and supply management before considering some contemporary issues in retailing. The next area of your studies in Block 3 is retail marketing.

Block learning outcomes

Now that you have completed all the multimedia activities and the reading related to Block 2 you should be able to:

- understand and explain some of the retail-specific management issues, techniques, roles and functions relevant to in-store operations.

You have developed your learning by:

- gaining experience in the selection, analysis and critical use of relevant retail information to make comparisons between practice
- gaining experience and understanding of how to frame and address problems, questions and issues related to in-store retailing
- applying problem-solving skills through the critical appraisal of human resource, customer service and customer relationship management theory and professional retailing practices

- continuing to work with others in your tutor group forum
- drawing on and using, as appropriate, relevant management and retail theory and techniques.

You have now reached the end of Book 2. You should now complete the TMA for Block 2.

References

Alpha Keeper Product Catalog (2009) [online], http://www.sellmore.nl/pdf/Keepers_Product_Catalog.pdf (Accessed 9 June 2010).

Anderson, C. H. (1984) 'Job design: employee satisfaction and performance in retail stores', *Journal of Small Business Management*, vol. 22, no. 4, pp. 9–16.

Broadbridge, A. and Parsons, E. (2003) 'United Kingdom charity retailing: managing in a newly professionalised sector', *Journal of Marketing Management*, vol. 19, nos 7–8, pp. 729–48.

Carlzon, J. (1987) *Moments of Truth*, New York, HarperCollins.

Cater, B. and Zabkar, V. (2008), 'Antecedents and consequences of commitment in marketing research services: the client's perspective', *Industrial Marketing Management*, vol. 38, no. 7, pp 785–97.

Chapman, P. and Templar, S. (2006) 'Scoping the contextual issues that influence shrinkage measurement', *International Journal of Retail & Distribution Management*, vol. 34, no. 11, pp. 860–72.

CIPD (2010) [online], http://www.cipd.co.uk/subjects/empreltns/psycntrct/psycontr.htm?IsSrchRes=1 (Accessed 22 October 2010).

Cox, R. and Brittain, P. (2003) *Retailing: an Introduction*, Prentice Hall, Harlow, England.

Emberson, C., Storey, J., Godsell, J. and Harrison, A. (2006) 'Managing the supply chain using in-store supplier employed merchandisers', *International Journal of Retail & Distribution Management*, vol. 34, no. 6, pp. 467–81.

Esbjerg, L., Buck, N. and Grunert, K. G. (2010) 'Making working in retailing interesting: a study of human resource management practices in danish grocery retail chains', *Journal of Retailing and Consumer Services*, vol. 17, no. 2, pp. 97–108.

Ford, W. S. Z. (2001) 'Customer expectations for interactions with service providers: relationship versus encounter orientation and personalized service communication', *Journal of Applied Communication Research*, vol. 29, no. 1, pp. 1–29.

Fornell, C. and Wernerfelt, B. (1987) 'Defensive marketing strategy by customer complaint management: a theoretical analysis', *Journal of Marketing Research*, vol. 24, no. 4, pp. 337–46.

Ganesh, J., Reynolds, K. E. and Luckett, M. G. (2007) 'Retail patronage behaviour and shopper typologies: a replication and extension using a multi-format, multi-method approach', *Journal of the Academy of Marketing Science*, vol. 35, no. 3, pp. 369–81.

Hackman, J. R. and Oldham, G. R. (1980) *Work Redesign*, Boston, MA., Addison-Wesley.

Herzberg, F., Maunser, B. and Snyderman, B. (1959) *The Motivation to Work*, Wiley, New York.

Jobber, D. (2010) *Principles and Practice of Marketing* (6th edn), McGraw-Hill.

Johnson, L. (2008) 'So you want to work in… confectionery', *Guardian*, 25 October [online], http://www.guardian.co.uk/education/2008/oct/25/graduate-confectionery-food-drink (Accessed 22 October 2010).

Kerfoot, S., Davies, B. and Ward, P. (2003) 'Visual merchandising and the creation of discernible retail brands', *International Journal of Retail & Distribution Management*, vol. 31, no. 3, pp. 143–52.

Kirn, S. P., Rucci, A. J., Huselid, M. A. and Becker, B. E. (1999) 'Strategic human resource management at Sears', *Human Resource Management*, vol. 38, no. 4 (winter), pp. 329–35.

Lea-Greenwood, G. (1998) 'Visual merchandising: a neglected area in UK fashion marketing?', *International Journal of Retail & Distribution Management*, vol. 26, no. 8, pp. 324–329.

Maslow, A. H. (1943) 'A theory of human motivation', *Psychological Review*, vol. 50, pp. 370–96.

Mauri, C. (2003) 'Card loyalty: a new emerging issue in grocery retailing', *Journal of Retailing*, vol. 10, pp. 13–25.

McGregor, D. C. (1989) *The Human Side of Enterprise*, New York, McGraw-Hill.

Morgan, M. R. and Hunt, S. D. (1994) 'The commitment-trust theory of relationship marketing', *Journal of Marketing*, vol. 58, no. 7, pp. 20–38.

Mutch, A. (2008) *Managing Information and Knowledge in Organizations: A Literacy Approach*, New York, Routledge, Taylor & Francis Group.

Parasuraman, A., Zeithaml, V. A. and Berry, L. L. (1985) 'A conceptual model of service quality and its implications for future research', *Journal of Marketing*, vol. 49, no. 4, pp. 41–50.

Parasuraman, A., Zeithaml, V. A. and Berry, L. L. (1990) 'SERVQUAL: a multiple-item scale for measuring consumer perceptions of service quality', *Journal of Retailing*, vol. 64, no. 1, pp. 12–40.

Parsons, E. (2002) 'Charity retail: past, present and future', *International Journal of Retail & Distribution Management*, vol. 30, no. 12, pp. 586–94.

Parsons, E. and Broadbridge, A. (2006) 'Job motivation and satisfaction: unpacking the key factors for charity shop managers', *Journal of Retailing and Consumer Services*, vol. 13, no. 3, pp. 121–31.

Payne, S. C., Horner, M. T., Boswell, W. R., Schroeder, A. N. and Stine-Cheyne, K. J. (2009) 'Comparison of online and traditional performance appraisal systems', *Journal of Managerial Psychology*, vol. 24, no. 6, pp. 526–44.

Purcell, J. and Kinnie, N. (2007) 'HRM and business performance' in Boxall, P., Purcell, J. and Wright, P. (eds) *The Oxford Handbook of Human Resource Management*, Oxford, Oxford University Press.

Roberts, R. (2007) 'Motivation and the self' in Knights, D. and Willmott, H. (eds) *Introducing Organizational Behaviour and Management*, London, Thomson Learning.

Rowley, J. (2005) 'Customer knowledge management or customer surveillance', *Global Business and Economics Review*, vol. 7, no. 1, pp. 100–10.

Rucci, A. J., Kirn, S. P. and Quinn, R. T. (1998) 'The employee–customer–profit chain at Sears', *Harvard Business Review*, January–February, pp. 83–97.

SecurityPark.net (2008) 'Alpha Keeper system reduces razor blade shrinkage' [online], http://www.securitypark.co.uk/security_article261729.html (Accessed 9 June 2010).

Singh, J. (1988) 'Consumer complaint intentions and behaviour: definitional and taxonomical issues', *Journal of Marketing*, vol. 52, no. 1, pp. 93–107.

Smith, A. D. (2010) 'Retail-based loyalty card programmes and CRM concepts: an empirical study', *International Journal of Innovation and Learning*, vol. 7, no. 3, pp. 303–30.

Varley, R. and Rafiq, M. (2004) *Principles of Retail Management*, Basingstoke, Palgrave Macmillan.

Watson, E. (2005) 'Tesco throws down the gauntlet' [online], http://www.foodmanufacture.co.uk/news/fullstory.php/aid/1350/Tesco_throws_down_gauntlet.html (Accessed 5 January 2010).

Zablah, A. R., Bellenger, D. N. and Johnston, W. J. (2004) 'An evaluation of divergent perspectives on customer relationship management: towards a common understanding of an emergent phenomenon', *Industrial Marketing Management*, vol. 33, no. 6, pp. 475–89.

Acknowledgements

Text

Box 3.1: © The Times 100 and MBA Publishing Ltd (www.thetimes100.co.uk).

Boxes 4.1 and 4.2 and Table 4.2: Rosemary Varley and Mohammed Rafiq, *Principles of Retail Management*, published 2003. Palgrave Macmillan. Reproduced with permission of Palgrave Macmillan.

Box 5.1: Watson, E. (2005) 'Tesco throws down the gauntlet', www.foodmanufacture.co.uk. © William Reed Business Media Ltd.

Box 5.2: www.SecurityPark.net (2008) 'Alpha Keeper system reduces razor blade shrinkage', www.SecurityPark.net, 4 July. With kind permission.

Case study 5.1: Rowley, J (2005) 'Customer knowledge management or consumer surveillance', *Global Business and Economic Review,* vol. 7, 2005, Inderscience Enterprises Ltd.

Page 22: Ford, L (2008) 'So you want to work in... confectionery', *Guardian*, 25 October 2008. Copyright © Guardian News and Media Ltd 2008.

Figures

Figure 4.1: Parasuraman, A et al. (1985) 'A conceptual model of service quality and its implications for future research', *Journal of Marketing*, vol. 49, no. 4, 1985, American Marketing Association.

Figure 4.2: Singh, J (1988) 'Consumer complaint intentions and behavior: definitional and texonomical issues', *Journal of Marketing*, vol. 52, Janaury 1988, American Marketing Association.

Figure 4.3: Rucci, A. (1998) 'The employee-customer-profit chain at Sears', *Harvard Business Review*, January–February. Harvard Business School Publishing.

Illustrations

Covers: Adapted from 3D images supplied by 3DStudio and Turbosqid.

Page 10: © Lightworks Media/Alamy.

Page 13: © Bonnie Jacobs, iStockphoto.

Page 16: © Richard Duszczak. www.cartoonstudio.co.uk.

Page 26: © Bloomberg/Getty Images.

Page 29: © Justin Kase z02z/Alamy.

Module team

The Module Team

Fiona Ellis-Chadwick *(Module Team Chair and author)*
Caroline Emberson *(Author)*
Roshan Boojihawon *(Author)*
Leslie Budd *(Reader in Social Enterprise, OUBS)*
Michael Phillips *(Group Regional Manager, Undergraduate Programme)*
Frances Myers *(Regional Manager)*
Erica Youngman *(Programme Coordinator)*
Colin Stanton *(Curriculum Manager)*
Iris Widdows *(Curriculum Manager)*
Pat McCarthy *(Qualification Manager)*
Val O'Connor *(Module Team Assistant)*
Sue Treacy *(Module Team Assistant)*

Other contributors

Diane Preston, Open University Business School
Mohammed Rafiq, Loughborough University Business School
Keith Pond, Loughborough University Business School
Christopher Moore, Caledonian Business School

Critical Readers

Haider Ali
Kristen Reid
Sue Hughes
Joan Hunt
Sally Booker
Rob Parker
Jerome Kiley
Noreen Siddiqui
Terry Robinson
John Pal
Paul Cowell

External Assessor

Professor Peter Jones, Department of Business, Education and Professional Studies, University of Gloucestershire

Production Team

Jodie Archbold *(Picture Researcher and Rights Clearances Assistant)*
Jill Alger *(Editor)*
Martin Brazier *(Graphic Designer)*
Johanna Breen *(Editorial Media Developer)*
Anne Brown *(Media Assistant)*

Angela Davies (*Media Assistant*)
Vicky Eves (*Graphic Artist*)
Chris French (*Producer for Sound and Vision*)
Sara Hack (*Graphic Artist*)
Lucy Hendy (*Media Assistant*)
Diane Hopwood (*Picture Researcher and Rights Clearances Assistant*)
Chris Hough (*Graphic Designer*)
Lee Johnson (*Media Project Manager*)
Edwina Jones (*Editorial Media Developer*)
Jane Roberts (*Producer for Sound and Vision*)
Kelvin Street (*Librarian*)
Keith Wakeman (*Online Service Administrator*)

Video assets

Nigel Douglas (*Executive Creative Director*)
Robin Tucker (*Head of Production*)

Consultants

James McGill *(Figure descriptions)*
Paul Meakin *(Adviser on Law)*